D0598464

Early Intervention Games

Early Intervention Games

Fun, Joyful Ways to Develop Social and Motor
Skills in Children with Autism Spectrum or
Sensory Processing Disorders

BARBARA SHER

ILLUSTRATIONS BY
RALPH BUTLER

JOSSEY-BASS
A Wiley Imprint
www.josseybass.com

Copyright © 2009 by John Wiley & Sons, Inc. All rights reserved.

Published by Jossey-Bass

A Wiley Imprint

989 Market Street, San Francisco, CA 94103-1741—www.josseybass.com

No part of this publication may be reproduced, stored in a retrieval system, or transmitted in any form or by any means, electronic, mechanical, photocopying, recording, scanning, or otherwise, except as permitted under Section 107 or 108 of the 1976 United States Copyright Act, without either the prior written permission of the publisher, or authorization through payment of the appropriate per-copy fee to the Copyright Clearance Center, Inc., 222 Rosewood Drive, Danvers, MA 01923, 978-750-8400, fax 978-646-8600, or on the Web at www.copyright.com. Requests to the publisher for permission should be addressed to the Permissions Department, John Wiley & Sons, Inc., 111 River Street, Hoboken, NJ 07030, 201-748-6011, fax 201-748-6008, or online at www.wiley.com/go/permissions.

Readers should be aware that Internet Web sites offered as citations and/or sources for further information may have changed or disappeared between the time this was written and when it is read.

Limit of Liability/Disclaimer of Warranty: While the publisher and author have used their best efforts in preparing this book, they make no representations or warranties with respect to the accuracy or completeness of the contents of this book and specifically disclaim any implied warranties of merchantability or fitness for a particular purpose. No warranty may be created or extended by sales representatives or written sales materials. The advice and strategies contained herein may not be suitable for your situation. You should consult with a professional where appropriate. Neither the publisher nor author shall be liable for any loss of profit or any other commercial damages, including but not limited to special, incidental, consequential, or other damages.

Jossey-Bass books and products are available through most bookstores. To contact Jossey-Bass directly call our Customer Care Department within the U.S. at 800-956-7739, outside the U.S. at 317-572-3986, or fax 317-572-4002.

Jossey-Bass also publishes its books in a variety of electronic formats. Some content that appears in print may not be available in electronic books.

Library of Congress Cataloging-in-Publication Data

Sher, Barbara.
    Early intervention games : fun, joyful ways to develop social and motor skills in children with autism, spectrum, or, sensory processing disorders / Barbara Sher.
        p.   cm.
    Includes bibliographical references and index.
        ISBN 978-0-470-39126-6 (pbk.)
        1. Autistic children. 2. Children with disabilities—Development. 3. Motor ability in children. 4. Social skills in children. I. Title.
    RJ506.A9S526 2009
        649'.154—dc22

                                                                              2009023238

Printed in the United States of America
FIRST EDITION
PB Printing   10 9 8 7 6 5 4 3 2 1

Contents - - - - - - - - - - - - - - - - - - -

CHAPTER 4 Social Fine Motor Games   117

CHAPTER 5 Water Games

Preface

Attitudes toward autism have gone through many changes. In my first twenty years as an occupational therapist, I had two clients with Autism Spectrum Disorder (ASD). They were considered exotic birds; their rocking, spinning, and hand flapping were called "self-stimming;" and their behavior was blamed squarely on the coldness of their "refrigerator moms."

Now, these once atypical children are common in my caseload, and self-stimulating behavior is more accurately acknowledged as self-calming. Instead of being blamed, their moms are honored for their ability to cope with their sensitive children.

The jury is still out on the cause of autism, but what is apparent is that the brains of these children process information differently. Now that we understand the plasticity of the brain, modern therapies are aimed toward helping these children connect the dots in ways that other children do, so they can better fit into our world.

There are even people nowadays who propose that children on the spectrum and with Sensory Processing Disorders (SPD) are more rather than advanced less than their peers. A growing awareness of autistic savants, with genius mixed into their social differences, adds some muscle to that theory.

It's an interesting thought. I think of Reggie, one of "my" kids. I was watching him blow bubbles recently and saw him mesmerized by the way the light refracted off the iridescent bubbles. If you really pay attention, bubbles *are* amazingly beautiful, and Reggie was just as delighted and appreciative of the fortieth bubble blown as he was of the first. (Talk about being in the present moment!) Reggie's ability to notice details also makes him the only one in his preschool class to know the names and sounds of every letter in the alphabet. I envy his contentment in solitary play and his not seeming to care or notice what others think of him.

What would it be like if kids like Reggie were just seen as one in a variety of human possibilities? I won't be surprised if sometime in the not too distant future, it might be considered "cool" to be autistic or to have unique ways of processing the world. Such terms as Sensory Processing Differences will be used instead of Disorders, and we *all* will learn to be sensitive to our needs and how to regulate and calm our systems.

Meanwhile, we parents and therapists and friends who love these children can make them feel welcomed and find ways to help them acquire needed skills. One way will always be playing. Play is the brain's way of learning and our way to enjoy our lives and to give love to each other. Daniel Tammet, an autistic savant points out in his book, *Born on a Blue Day*, that what made his childhood miserable were the children who couldn't accept him as he was, but what made his development flourish were his parents who did.

May the games in this book bring you and yours many loving, playful moments.

Barbara Sher

Acknowledgments ·- - - ~ ~ - ~ ~ - ~ ~

It's one thing to come up with games to play with children and another to find a staff willing to play with you. Playing requires willingness to break into song at any moment and being alert, innovative, and flexible to each child's unique needs. Our Early Childhood and Special Education staff of aides, teachers, and therapists in the CNMI public school system feel so good about the progress we've seen in "our" children that we modestly call ourselves the Dream Team.

To honor our staff's playfulness and competence, I dedicate this book to them. It was their willingness to happily play every game, many times, which gave me the ability to make games that work best.

Thank you, Joe Cruz, Yoli Lely, Mercy Tisa, Melinda Diaz, Jacob Villagomez, Mark and Patty Staal, Jerry and Rose Diaz, Dora Won, and Judy Hawkins, and helpers, Rita Olipai and Reyda Calibo.

I also want to express special appreciation to early intervention teacher Mark Staal, who had the vision and was instrumental in setting up the local program for children with ASD and SPD. He and Jerry Diaz made important suggestions about aspects to include in the book.

Huge acknowledgment also goes to fellow occupational therapist and dear friend, Karen Beardsley. Karen has a wide range of therapeutic experience, and I was thrilled when she agreed to be my first reader. She assiduously went through the text and, in her characteristically intelligent style, added a sentence, a thought, or a clearer articulation of a therapeutic intervention. For this, I'm very grateful.

Along with Karen's, I received helpful feedback from Carol Kranowitz and Mary Sue Williams, both authors and outstanding professionals in the field. Their comments were invaluable.

I also truly appreciate Kate Bradford, my editor, who did her usual meticulous and thoughtful tidying and rearranging to add the spit and polish to my vision.

And always I'm grateful to my illustrator, Ralph Butler, who knows to include the wide swath of cultures in his lively illustrations. He knows how to exemplify so clearly in pictures what I say in words.

I appreciate the strong support given to me by my new friend and kindred soul, Ida Zelaya. With her pulse on parental needs through her sensorystreet.com Web site, she understands the power of play with children who have sensory processing differences and shares my words with other parents.

My appreciation wholeheartedly extends to the people in my life who have always given me love, applause, and unending encouragement—my family. My daughters, Roxanne and Marissa, are my continual source of joy, including their husbands, Ehren and Mark, and, especially, my grandson Oliver. I so appreciate my brother Monty and sister-in-law Glo my sisters Bonnie and Trisha, and brother-in-law David, my stepdaughter Jessica, and Stuart, Max, and Griff. Also, sweet thanks to my Mom and, in spirit, my Dad and my Richard. I adore them all.

It takes a gazillion hours to birth a book, and each time I'm finished, I forget, like a woman after labor is over, how much effort it "was . . . until" I have already joyously begun the next book. It's easy to see why I'm especially glad for my loving partner and favorite playmate, Don Cohen, who keeps me company and well fed when I'm writing and joins me on fun outings when I'm not. He is a joy and a comfort for me, and I am deeply appreciative and pleased.

Early Intervention Games

Introduction - - - - - - - - - - - - - - -

Kids who are diagnosed with an Autism Spectrum Disorder (ASD) or Sensory Processing Disorder (SPD) come in all shapes, sizes, and strengths. Like children everywhere, they are all uniquely themselves, with their own preferences, their own needs, and their own sensitivities. A difference between typically developing children and these children is that children with ASD or SPD let you know, without a doubt, what their preferences, needs, and sensitivities are. They wear their needs on their sleeves.

If Joseph doesn't like loud noises, you know it. Maybe he will quietly put his hands over his ears, but he's just as likely to have a screaming meltdown. If Jason doesn't want to be disturbed and prefers to be left doing what he's doing, you're going to have a hard row to hoe getting him to do what you want. Susie doesn't like to be touched and she's not kidding. You get the idea. Typical children might be more willing to go along with your program, even if it's not their first choice, partly because they want to please or get praised. Children identified with autism spectrum or sensory integration issues can't always let your needs override theirs. If you want peace, you must pay attention to their needs. The challenge for parents, therapists, and others, including the child, is to figure out what the needs are.

You need to notice many things, such as:

Is there a sensation alarming my child and can it be modified or overridden by another sensation?
What in the environment is setting my child off and can I change it?
Is there something in his diet that has a negative effect on him?
What is her emotional state and how can I help calm her?

Can I help him cope by desensitizing, modifying, overriding, or avoiding something?

Would it be more helpful to distract my child's attention from her
anxiety by helping her focus on something that calms her, or to
change the situation?

We also need to notice and pay attention to ourselves. We all know what
it feels like to not be able to think clearly because the radio is too loud, or to
feel irritated by glaring headlights, or overwhelmed and even frightened by
a jostling crowd. Usually, we are able to block out annoying sensations and
focus on what is in front of us, but not always. Understanding the effects
of such assaults on our sensory system helps us to have more compassion
for the many people who can't tune them out and thus react negatively. To
paraphrase the Serenity Prayer, we need to learn to control the sensations
we can, avoid the ones we can't, and develop the wisdom to know the difference.

We need to learn to help those who can't do this by noticing their reactions to different stimuli and, when wanting assistance, to seek out intervention by occupational therapists or other professionals trained in treating
sensory issues. Understanding of the child's needs is increased when parents, family members, therapists, and the educational team can brainstorm
together and share their insights.

If there could be said to be a silver lining in this sudden increase in
the incidence of autism and SPD, then it must be that we're producing a
large group of parents and professionals who are increasingly sensitive to
the needs of children. As this awareness grows, this increased knowledge is
spreading. People are sharing their ideas in the neighborhood, in magazines
and books, and on the Web. More people are understanding and trying new
ways to help their youngster modify, cope, and deal with the world so that
joy, not pain, is the main sensation of their lives.

Besides enlarging our sensitivity, these children are influencing one of
the main challenges of this point in our history: accepting diversity. We're
working on accepting diversity in terms of religion, ethnicity, and sexual

orientation. People are now beginning to call for a greater acceptance of neurological diversity.

Zosia Zaks, an adult on the autism spectrum and the author of *Life and Love: Positive Strategies for Autistic Adults*, adds to this perspective, writing on her Web site (www.autismability.com):

> Most Autistic people do not want to be "cured" per se. We do not want our Autism magically erased, or erased over time via some method. You would wind up washing away who we are. This is important to understand. Many people across the spectrum, with a wide range of skills, talents, challenges, issues, and interests, are speaking out for a new understanding, are working hard to promote the benefits of neurological diversity. The goal should never be to make an Autistic person "normal" or "typical" or "just like his peers" because Autism is biological—neurological—and therefore Autistic people will always "be built" Autistic. Instead, try to work with us, as we are, so we can learn new skills, communicate, and enjoy our lives.

She also points out the importance of appreciating strengths:

> For example, many of us absolutely love color. We can have strong aesthetic ideals. Some of us are entranced by sounds, textures, and images and this leads to an amazing depth of artistic talent in our community. Think of Einstein standing there "stimming out" visually on the trains that gave him the idea for relativity. Many of our sensory-bound challenges mirror sensory-bound insights that can have incredible impacts on art, science, music, and engineering.

Daniel Hawthorne, another adult with autism, says in his book, *A Reason for Hope*, "There are two things I would want to tell parents. One is to be attentive to helping their children work from their strengths, using their own unique talents to meet life's challenges, rather than trying to constantly compensate for their weaknesses. Everyone has his own unique strengths and weaknesses, and autistic individuals are no different. If they can learn how to best use their unique strengths, then they will live happier lives for it."

I hope that the ideas in this book give you more ways to help children enjoy their lives and their own unique strengths.

The Games

The games in this book can be done in a classroom with many kids of different abilities, at home with one child and a parent, or with friends and siblings. Some of the aquatic therapy games can be done with just a water table or kiddie pool, but a few require a real pool, lake, or ocean. Some of the aquatic games can also be done on land instead.

Each game has the format described below:

TITLE

Some titles are chosen because they explain the game, as in Blanket Ride, and others because they are cute (if you think A Kid Sandwich is cute). Feel free to change the name to fit your group. Some names can be changed to be more appropriate for different cultures. For example, Sushi Roll gives an Asian flavor whereas Burrito Roll would make a clearer image in a Latin culture.

GOALS

This section lists the social, motor, and cognitive goals being encouraged, as well as the sensory system being stimulated.

MATERIALS

This section lists any material needed for the games. All of the materials are easy to find, and include recyclables.

SETUP

This section describes the kinds of things to do or to have ready to make the game go smoothly—For example, if children and adults need to be in a circle, or whether you need to have a pile of shoes nearby.

DIRECTIONS

This Explains how the game is played.

VARIATIONS

Variations can include different materials to use or other skills to be developed.

WHAT IS BEING LEARNED

This explains the various lessons that are being addressed.

MODIFICATIONS

This section suggests ways to modify the game to help children with specific abilities or sensitivities.

Individualizing the games maximizes your child's social success because you modify games according to your child's learning profile and skill level. One way to create a profile for your child is to use a Social Skills Profile, such as the easy-to-use one provided in an excellent resource, *Building Bridges Through Sensory Integration* (see the bibliography at the end of the book). This, along with continuing observations, gives you a picture of the child's skills so you can see how you might modify the game.

For example, Lenny's profile indicated that he

1. Avoids playing near other children

2. Wants to be in control

3. Seeks out deep pressure, hugs, excessive movement, frequent jumping and banging into things

4. Has a tendency to stare off into space

5. Has limited visual tracking and does not use his eyes to guide movement

6. Is oversensitive to the sounds of others and often covers his ears

In playing the boisterous game below with Lenny, modifications had to be made at first until the game had been played often enough to become familiar and comfortable. With the initial modifications, the game does not alert his defenses and he can begin with a positive, nonthreatening experience.

The Game: Throw the Balls into the Box

In this game, children gather around a cardboard box on the floor (with its flaps open on the bottom). Each child is given a ball to throw in the box as the group sings to the tune of "London Bridge Is Falling Down":

> Throw the ball into the box
> Into the box
> Into the box
> Throw the ball into the box
> Where did the ball go?

Then, when all the balls are in the box, say, "Are they *behind* the box?" (exaggerate looking behind the box); "Are they *beside* the box?" (again, exaggerate looking beside the box); "Are they *in* the box?" (then pick up the box, and since the bottom flaps are loose, all the balls fall out!).

Children are delighted by the surprise of the balls falling out and are excited to grab a ball and do it again, but some children need the activity modified.

The following modifications to the game could be made to fit Lenny's profile.

1. Avoids playing near other children

    When playing a variation of the game where children take turns, let him throw first so he can then back away from the group into a more comfortable space.

Make a stool available for him to use if he wants to be away from the group but still see what is going on.

Give him direct feedback that specifically describes things he did well to reinforce a positive sense of self. The more comfortable he gets in his own skin, the easier it is to be with others.

2. Wants to be in control

Let him have some time with his favorite toy after he first throws the ball.

During some of the group playtime, follow his lead. For example, if you know he loves airplanes, make paper airplanes and let him and the others throw them into the box instead of balls.

As he becomes more at ease, let him sometimes be the one who gets to lift the box at the end and shake the balls loose.

If he is having a bad day and wants total control and refuses to play, make sure he either stays and watches one game or does one action and then uses his words to say, "I want to go." When he does this, hug him goodbye (if he likes hugs) and allow him to go play with his favorite toy nearby.

3. Seeks out deep pressure, hugs, excessive movement, frequent jumping and banging into things

Give him a congratulatory hug every time he throws the ball in the box.

When he is standing in the crowd, give him a deep-pressure, comforting touch to his shoulders and upper arms.

Give him a weighted vest or other compression orthotic to wear.

4. Has a tendency to stare off into space and tune out

Cover the box in a bright color and sparkle it up to gain his attention.

Position him so that he can see the group leader and the box better.

Use his favorite things to bring him back to the here and now. For example, if he loves Spiderman, let him pretend to be Spiderman as he participates in the game.

5. Has limited visual tracking and does not use his eyes to guide movement

> Verbally encourage him to look at the box when he is throwing and sometimes do a hand-over-hand prompting. Later this can be reduced to just a simple touch prompt with a gestural cue.

> You could also try using a made-up hand signal or signing along with speaking to reinforce his vision.

6. Is oversensitive to the sounds of others and often covers his ears

> Until he gets used to the game, keep the singing soft or have the kids quietly take turns throwing.

Sometimes use the games as a starting point. If your child is throwing at a bowl in the Target Game and starts to throw the ball high in the air, modify the game to a basketball game. Lift the bowl high and have kids take turns making the basket. Or have one child toss the ball up, and you or another can have fun trying to catch it in the bowl on its way down.

For many more ideas on strategies and activities, see Appendix II and the Bibliography, where you'll find some wonderful, user-friendly books, Web sites, and listservs, such as Carol Kranowitz's *The Out-of-Sync Child Has Fun: Activities for Kids with Sensory Processing Disorder*; Dr. Lucy Miller's *Sensational Kids*; Mary Sue William and Sherry Shellenberger's Alert Program; *Tools for Tots: Sensory Strategies for Toddlers and Preschoolers* by Diana Henry et al.; and Ida Zelaya's www.sensorystreet.com Web site where parents trade ideas.

CHAPTER 1

- ~ - ~ - ~ -

Understanding Sensory Processing Issues

Sensory integration is an important consideration when working with children with Sensory Processing Disorder or sensory processing problems. Research shows that the majority of children on the autistic spectrum also have sensory problems, especially with hearing, touch, and vision. It's estimated that there is one child with sensory issues in every regular classroom, and somewhere between 50 and 80 percent of children have some degree of sensory problems in a classroom of children with Autism Spectrum Disorders.

Sensory processing is the ability of the brain to correctly integrate information brought in by the senses. The information we take in through the senses of touch, movement, smell, taste, vision, and hearing are combined with prior information, memories, and knowledge already stored in the brain to make sense of our world. In people without Sensory Processing Disorders, all the sensory input from the environment and all the input from our bodies work together seamlessly so we know what's going on and what to do. Without conscious effort, we are filtering out sensations that are not important.

Sensory processing occurs first by registration, when the child becomes aware of the sensation. The second stage is orientation, which enables the child to pay attention to the sensation. Next comes interpretation; the child has to somehow understand the information coming in. Finally comes organization, when the child uses the information to elicit a response. This can be an emotional behavior, a physical action, or a cognitive response.

Sensory Processing Disorder

When sensory input is not integrated or organized appropriately in the brain, children experience the world differently. They're not always getting an accurate, reliable picture of their bodies and the environment, and this misperception produces varying degrees of problems in development, information processing, and behavior. Because they are not always able to process information received through the senses, they cannot easily adapt to a situation. The neurobiology of the sensory systems is dysfunctional and therefore distorts the individual's ability to perceive the world correctly. People must be able to perceive, interpret, and process information so that they can learn about the world around them. If they are unable to do so, they can feel uncomfortable, which may show itself in such behaviors as tuning out or hand flapping.

Children with Sensory Processing Disorder may have difficulty "reading cues," either verbal or nonverbal, from the environment. Dysfunction in this area makes it difficult for people to adapt to their environment and function as others do. They may be hypersensitive to sound or touch, or unable to screen out distracting noises or clothing textures. Their response to these stimuli might be impulsive motor acts, making noises, or running away.

This hypersensitivity is also known as overresponsivity or sensory defensiveness. Children with this response may complain about how clothing feels, the annoyance of a tag, or how their socks have to be on just so. They could be picky eaters and get stuck on one certain food, making it impossible to get them to eat anything else. They might walk on their toes to avoid sensory input from the bottoms of their feet. They may not be able to tolerate normal lighting in a room. They may be so oversensitive to smells that, for example, a trip past the meat department at a supermarket is unbearable. Some children are oversensitive to sounds and will frequently cover their ears, even when listening to what is generally perceived as a pleasant sound. They usually feel uncomfortable with the noise in a group setting and often tune out. Children who are hypersensitive are on alert to protect themselves from real or imagined dangers in an unpredictable world. Their behavior might seem anxious, self-absorbed, or stubborn because the imagined danger is very real to them.

Children with sensory processing problems might also have the opposite response and be underresponsive. This hyposensitivity is characterized by an unusually high tolerance for environmental stimuli. Rather than avoiding smells, they seek to increase them by sniffing people, objects, and food. Rather than avoiding touch or touching, they will constantly be crashing into things or stamping their feet, seeking extra stimulation. Rather than avoiding motion and fatiguing easily, they may excessively crave intense movement and love to spin, swing, and jump, and can be in constant motion. They may get dizzy easily—or never at all. They may appear restless and be overactive because they are hyporesponsive and are trying to increase their alertness by seeking out sensory stimulation. When children are hyporesponsive to sensations, they are not defensive enough and are more likely to do things that put them in harm's way, such as running into the street or jumping from high places. They often have a high pain threshold and can become injured and not realize it.

In addition, some children may fluctuate between these extremes. Their arousal level is erratic and not necessarily relevant to the stimuli itself. This means that it would be very hard to predict how they might react.

As Carol Kranowitz points out in her book, *The Out-of-Sync Child* (2005, p. 78), "The child may be both over-responsive and under-responsive in one sensory system, or may be over-responsive to one kind of sensation and under-responsive to another, or may respond differently to the same stimulus depending on the time and context, fluctuating back and forth. Yesterday, after a long recess, he may have coped well with a fire alarm; today, when recess is cancelled, he may have a meltdown when a door clicks shut. Context makes a huge difference."

Types of Sensory Processing Disorders

Stanley I. Greenspan, MD and Lucy J. Miller, PhD, OTR further delineate sensory integration issues into categories. Sensory Processing Disorder is being used as a global umbrella term that includes all forms of this disorder, including three primary diagnostic groups.

TYPE I. SENSORY MODULATION DISORDER (SMD)

Sensory modulation refers to the process by which messages from the sensory system convey information about the intensity, frequency, duration, complexity, and novelty of sensory stimuli. Usually we respond with an appropriately graded reaction, neither underreacting nor overreacting.

Miller, in her book *Sensational Kids*, describes Sensory Modulation Disorder (SMD) as one that makes it hard for kids to match the intensity of their response to the intensity of the sensation. It takes the form of sensory overresponsivity which causes children to be more alert than most people. "Even when asleep, [their] 'engine' is running too fast, the way a car's engine does when the idle is set too high. This causes sounds and other sensations to seem more intense . . . than they would to a typically developing child. Even something as innocent as . . . [a door] slamming can jolt [a child] into instant and complete alertness the way a big BOOM coming from the furnace room of the house would alarm you or me" (p. 98).

Type II. Sensory-Based Motor Disorder (SBMD)

This dysfunction occurs when the sensory input of the proprioceptive and vestibular system is misinterpreted or incorrectly processed. The proprioceptive system lets us know what our body parts are doing, even in the dark when we can't see them, and how much strength we need to do specific tasks. The vestibular tells us if we are tilting or if our bodies are balanced. (Because the input from these systems is so crucial, they are a major factor in the design of the games in this book and are discussed in more detail below.)

When the child's central nervous system has difficulty making use of the sensory information from these systems, he can exhibit a subtype of SBMD called dyspraxia, which is the inability to carry out a sequence of actions that are necessary to do something the child wants to do, such as imitate actions, play sports, get on a bike, or climb a ladder. Children with SBMD are often clumsy, unintentionally breaking toys, or tripping over things. This may also show itself as a child who prefers sedentary fantasy play over playing sports.

Postural Disorder is another subtype whereby the child seems weak, tires easily, or doesn't consistently use a dominant hand or cross midline.

Type III. Sensory Discrimination Disorder (SDD)

This is the inability to distinguish between similar sensations. Sensory discrimination is the process whereby we take the information our senses deliver and we integrate, interpret, analyze, and associate it with all the data we have already stored, and make good use of the information. This enables us to know what is in our hands without looking, to find things by touch alone, to organize writing on a page, to differentiate between textures or smells, or to hear what is being said if there is background noise. This disorder can show itself as inattentiveness, disorganization, and poor school performance.

Sensory issues can be on a spectrum and as unique as fingerprints. Being annoyed by the scratchiness of a sweater is considered to be a typical sensory response for anyone. However, when a child is so strongly affected by tactile sensations or other sensory input that he totally withdraws, becomes hyperactive, or lashes out, the child's sensory issues are severe enough to warrant intervention.

The Three Major Sensory Systems

Dr. Jean Ayres, an occupational therapist, was the pioneer who formulated a theory of sensory integration that led to identification of Sensory Processing Disorders and to their therapeutic intervention.

In therapy, Ayres focuses primarily on three basic senses—tactile, vestibular, and proprioceptive. Although these three sensory systems are less familiar than vision and audition, they are critical, because they help us to experience, interpret, and respond to different stimuli in our environment. Their interconnections start forming before birth and continue to develop as the person matures and interacts with her environment. These three senses are not only interconnected but are also connected with other systems in the brain and will be discussed in detail below. Many of the motor activities used in the games in this book are designed to integrate, challenge, and stimulate these systems.

THE VESTIBULAR SYSTEM

The vestibular system is found in the inner ear (the semicircular canals) and detects movement and changes in the position of the head. It is how we relate in space. It is a foundation for muscle tone, balance, and bilateral coordination. All other types of sensation are processed according to vestibular information, so it is a unifying system in our brains.

Children who are hypersensitive to vestibular stimulation may have a "fight or flight" response that would cause them to be very frightened or want to run away or strike out at others. They may have a fearful reaction to ordinary movement activities and seem anxious in space and appear clumsy. They will shun playground equipment and riding in elevators or escalators, and sometimes even in cars. They may refuse to be picked up or to ever let their feet leave the ground.

Children with a hyporeactive vestibular system may purposefully seek excessive body movements, such as whirling, jumping, spinning, hanging upside down, swinging for long periods, constantly moving, or just continually fidgeting. They may rock when upset; this is a kind of tranquilizing self-therapy. They are trying continuously to stimulate their vestibular systems in order to achieve a state of quiet alertness.

Temple Grandin, whose landmark book, *Seeing in Pictures*, made her famous as one of the first people to write about having autism, invented a "squeeze machine." This machine put pressure on her trunk, similar to a firm hug, which brought her comfort and relief.

THE TACTILE SYSTEM

The tactile system is the largest sensory system in our body and is composed of receptors in the skin, which send information to the brain regarding such factors as light, touch, pain, temperature, and pressure. This input gives form to body and spatial awareness and plays an important role in perceiving the environment and in establishing protective reactions for survival. There are two components to the system: protective, which is defensive; and discriminative, which is discerning. These two must work together to enable us to function and perform everyday tasks.

Hypersensitivity in the tactile system, also called tactile defensiveness, may lead to a misperception of touch and can be seen in the affected child's withdrawing when being touched, avoiding groups, refusing to eat certain foods, wearing certain types of clothing, avoiding getting his hands dirty, or using his fingertips rather than whole hands to manipulate objects. The child with tactile dysfunction will often curl her hands into loose fists to avoid touching; keeping her hands in that position can affect her fine motor skills. This dysfunction may also display itself in behavior where children try to isolate themselves or are generally irritable. This is where you might see the "fight or flight" response.

Hyposensitivity is seen in children who are undersensitive or unaware of pain, temperature, or how some objects feel. Sometimes they seek more stimulation and may paw through toys, chew on objects, or bump into people or furniture. Painful tactile stimulation may not be felt, easily leaving the child defenseless or vulnerable to dangerous situations. Intervention needs to include intense touch stimulation to help them adequately process the information.

THE PROPRIOCEPTIVE SYSTEM

The proprioceptive system lies along muscle fibers and in the tendons and ligaments that provide a person with a subconscious awareness of body position and how it is moving. It allows us to automatically adjust in different situations, such as stepping off a curb, sitting in a chair, or staying upright on uneven surfaces. Even fine motor tasks, such as writing, using a soup spoon, or buttoning a shirt, depend on an efficient proprioceptive system. This system helps to develop adapted responses to our environment.

When the proprioceptive system is hypersensitive, there is difficulty receiving information from the muscles and joints. The affected person is unable to properly interpret the feedback about movement and will often have poor body awareness. Signs of dysfunction are clumsiness, a tendency to fall, odd body posturing, messy eating, and difficulty manipulating small objects, such as buttons and snaps. Children may put too much or too little pressure on objects and break toys without meaning to do so. They may resist new motor movement activities because they have been unsuccessful with imitating movements in the past.

Likewise there may be hyposensitivity, in which there is an underlying high pain threshold and the affected person needs more input to gain sensation. Behaviors seen may be excessive crashing or bumping into things, biting or teeth grinding, head banging, and so on.

Another dimension of proprioception is where we find the dyspraxia problems mentioned above. Praxis or motor planning is the ability to plan and execute different motor tasks, such as imitating another's movements, climbing a tree, or copying words from a blackboard. In order to do this, the system needs accurate information from the sensory system. The child with dyspraxia has difficulty using sensory information to plan and organize what needs to be done and may not learn easily.

VISUAL AND AUDITORY PROCESSING

In order to understand the children's reactions when we are playing games with them, we also need to understand something about problems with visual and auditory processing.

Visual processing deficits do not mean that those affected cannot see. Rather it means that their brains are not processing what they are seeing. It is a very complex system. If asked to go get an object, they might look right at it and then say they can't find it. They might also have a hard time finding the words for objects they are viewing. They may exhibit poor spatial awareness, lack coordination, and have overall learning problems as well. The vestibular system and vision work collaboratively in order to maintain posture and balance.

Similarly, auditory processing deficits are not about problems with hearing, but about processing the information heard. The child may hear what you say, but the brain may not integrate and assimilate your words. It's not that the child doesn't understand—it simply may take a moment or more before it clicks in.

Auditory processing has also been associated with the vestibular system. Some children may have auditory defensiveness and may become anxious or sensitive to certain sounds and frequencies. Likewise, they may be hyposensitive and find ways to seek out and repeat certain noises, or may fixate on them.

How Sensory Processing Disorders Affect Socialization

Sensory difficulties may show up in academic underachievement; problems with peer interaction, attention, gross and fine motor coordination, and activity level; developmental difficulties; poor self-esteem; and speech or language delays. Behaviors are almost always affected, and the child may be impulsive, aggressive, distractible, fearful, withdrawn, or "in his or her own world"; may show a general lack of planning, and may have difficulty adjusting to new situations.

Sensory Processing Disorders can take many forms, but almost always show up in social activities. What other children find enjoyable can be extremely uncomfortable for kids with sensory processing issues. Other children might be having fun playing ball in the field, trading gossip, and joyfully squealing or shouting. But for children with sensory issues, the playground can be an unpredictable, scary, confusing, and dangerous place. The noise levels are too loud, the visual clutter of running children is disorganizing, and the possibility of being bumped, or of even just inadvertently touching something, can be frightening. If being touched is an issue, if the sensory systems that give one a sense of balance and body awareness are not aligned, if being in crowds produces anxiety, then it makes sense that social situations would be difficult.

The child's social behavior may look "odd," "geeky," "babyish," or "weird." Children who are trying to protect themselves by stubbornly refusing to do things might be seen as "problem" kids with "an attitude." For example, if the child is trying to calm himself by flapping his hand or twirling, others might see him as odd and avoid his company. Or the child might be ostracized because she doesn't understand the rules of social space and, seeking sensory input, gets right into another's face, touches too much, or bumps into others too often.

Having trouble with transitions—going from one activity to the next— makes school routines a problem and may cause these children to act out, thus making them different from the others. You may see such social behaviors as anxiety, withdrawal, anger, defiance, and defensiveness, which make it difficult for children with Sensory Processing Disorders to be accepted by other children.

When sensory information is unpredictable, it's easy to see why some of these children prefer facts and information and putting objects in order. These things are completely stable and predictable and do not change according to one's arousal state.

CHAPTER 2

How the Games Help Sensory Processing Challenges

Carol Kranowitz, author of *The Out-of-Sync Child*, the popular book for parents on Sensory Processing Disorder, commented, "Until I learned about sensory integration dysfunction, I could not find a pattern in the children in my classroom that were different from the others. The only common thread—and this is what troubled me the most—was their sadness. Whether their modus operandi was hostility, aggression, anger, frustration, tuning-out, whining, silliness, or wildly inappropriate gusto, they all seemed to sense that they weren't like the other kids. They didn't feel a sense of belonging."

The games in this book are designed to address the sensory system and give children that sense of belonging. They are designed to help children develop motor skills so that they can be successful in the playground. They are planned to help children be more sensitive to some systems and less sensitive to others.

But mainly, the games are played so that these children can see that being with other people can be fun.

Goals and Methods of Early Intervention Games

Chris came into the school's playroom reluctantly. He tended to be reluctant about most activities in which he wasn't the initiator and showed his discomfort by standing by the glass door, with his back to us, looking out.

In the middle of the room was a huge cardboard box, and because it was an unusual thing to see in the classroom, we were able to persuade him to come over and have a look at it. He looked inside and then stood aside and watched as his schoolmate, Kaya, got placed inside the box. We loosely closed the top flaps and crooned, "Who's in the box? Who's in the box? Knock knock knock. Who's in the box?" We opened the flaps, Kaya popped her head out, and we said, "It's Kaya!" We gave Kaya and Jimmy and Damion turns while Chris watched and even knocked on the box.

"It's Chris's turn," we said enthusiastically, but not at all sure about how he would feel about getting in the box. To our delight, he let us put him inside and immediately sat down, so we closed the flaps. Again we crooned our tune and knocked softly on the box in case the noise would irritate him. When we opened the flaps, there he was with a huge grin on his face.

Chris wanted several more turns, and then was in such a good mood that he was willing to play the next game when we turned the box on its side, opened up all the flaps, and the children crawled through the "tunnel."

Chris and the others were at what we call "Social Club." The group is mainly made of Head Start preschool kids who have been diagnosed with Autism Spectrum Disorder or Sensory Processing Disorder, or both, but also includes children with other needs, and often a couple of typically developing children. Our classroom is set up with basic motor equipment, such as a small trampoline and balance beam, and other play materials, mostly things easily found or made. We start the session in a predictable pattern: first singing a couple of familiar songs, doing a jumping game, and going through the obstacle course. Then we introduce new games or variations of old games. For example, instead of getting or giving rides inside a box, the children get pulled or help pull others who are sitting on a blanket. Six or more gross motor games are followed by some fine motor activities. The class ends with the familiar goodbye song.

On another day of the week, the same gang meets, but this time at a pool for aquatic therapy. There we mix familiar activities with the new ones. We start the session in a small "hot tub" filled with lukewarm water and sing a variety of songs and play games. Then we move to the big pool to play more games. We end with the same familiar goodbye song.

Are the groups successful? Kids like Chris who were hesitant at first soon began to run to the classroom, excited to begin the sessions. Children who were initially fearful of the water began smiling when the school bus arrived at the pool site. The children, each in their own way and in their own time, began to get the underlying message: playing with others can be fun.

Major Goals of Games

Although each game has its individual set of goals, which are included in the descriptions of the specific games, there are three major goals for all the games.

The first is to encourage the ability to focus on the present moment. Children need to attend before they can play socially. There is a level of alert energy that needs to be attained before playing can take place. We know this from our own lives. If our energy is too low, we're not in the mood to be engaged with others. If our energy is too high, we're too jittery to focus and our attention is scattered. Mary Sue Williams and Sherry Shellenberger use the analogy of an engine in their Alert Program to help children understand the differences between an engine that is revving, sluggish, or idling nicely.

Children, especially those with hyperactivity, are said to have an "attention deficit." The more descriptive term would be "attention surplus." Sensory and kinesthetic information is coming in fast and furious without filtering as to which is relevant and which is not. Some children react by darting here and there and noticing it all. Others deal with the barrage of information by shutting down and ignoring it all. Our goal is to help the children find that middle ground of alert interest where they are not overwhelmed or underwhelmed. They need to be in the middle ground where they can see what is foreground, or information to notice, and what is background, or information to ignore. It is in this level of alertness that we can elicit "shared attention," when children are able to notice and interact with the same object.

The second major goal is to increase coordination, because one of the best ways to play and socially interact with others is to do something physical together. "Clumsy" is frequently used to describe many of the children on the spectrum and with sensory processing problems. The lack of fluid coordination is often a result of poor ideation and motor planning, which creates obstacles in executing movements. Difficulties with vestibular and proprioceptive systems contribute to poor balance and body awareness. Our goal, then, is to help the children develop the foundation for basic motor skills so that they can play with others. Through a variety of carefully selected games, and while addressing the hierarchical needs of their sensory systems, we help them develop the skills they need. We help them learn how to throw, jump, run, and stop on a dime so that they can play a variety of games.

The third and probably most important goal of therapy is for the kids to learn that it's worth it to pay attention and to engage in back-and-forth play. And as their coordination builds, so do their confidence and their desire to repeat these social experiences. The importance of practicing and mastering these skills in a safe haven is that the children will ultimately be able to transfer them to other situations and interactions outside the group and be able to have fun socializing and engaging with peers in the community. In Social Club and aquatic therapy, we want to put them in situations where they are enjoying themselves, and from this happier place, they can be open and less resistant to relating to others. Mainly, we want them to have the experiences that show them that relating to others can be fun!

Main Methods Used in the Games

To accomplish these goals, we use two main methods.

The first is to provide the appropriate stimulation for the children's sensory systems: visual, auditory, tactile, gustatory, proprioceptive, and vestibular. We then observe the actions or behaviors that the children exhibit from these systems in order to provide the "just right" input or challenge. Are their bodies off balance? Can they imitate movements? Do sights or sounds across the room distract them? Are they covering their ears? The games we select and play support these systems to increase the children's awareness of themselves and their peers. The feedback from these systems ultimately begins to help the children understand their surroundings and develop some mastery within their environment.

Exposing children to select sensory experiences can fulfill two opposite needs. The child who seeks sensory input by, for example, touching everything, will have his need honored and satiated by being exposed to a variety of textures. The child who is on the other extreme—hypersensitive to touch—will learn to begin to tolerate different textures by starting with what she can handle. For example, if she were reluctant to touch gooey stuff, such as glue, and needs to wash her hands incessantly, she would benefit by beginning to play with sticky labels or other mildly sticky substances. As the child's need for avoiding or seeking out extra stimulation decreases, his emotional energy is freed up and more available for socializing.

To be successful with this sensory approach, a second method is crucial: we need to respect and pay attention to each child's uniqueness. We need to have a sense of what kinds of activities calm them, which make them uncomfortable, and which interest them and increase their alertness. For example, is Joey spinning the wheel of the bike repeatedly because he needs to calm himself by focusing on only one aspect and in order to find predictability in his unpredictable world? If so, our emphasis would be on introducing him to other calming objects, such as kaleidoscopes and snow globes, and gentle movements to expand his repertoire of ways of dealing with the world.

Or maybe he is spinning the wheel because he would like to experience going in circles himself. We start slowly and gently finding out. He could easily be the kind of kid who turns out to love being swirled around because his system needs it. By making spinning into a game, he goes from solitary play to engaged fun with another.

If he is distressed from imagined dangers set off by the "fight or flight" brain stem response, it's our job to honor his feelings and help him find ways to cope and get relief. Familiarity and graded exposure would be among the techniques used to help him later.

Concurrent Therapies

Some of the requisites for playing social games are to be able to imitate the actions of others and to have receptive language, starting with understanding simple commands, such as "Come here," "Sit down," and "Do this." We help children to learn and practice these skills that reinforce the social skills of attending, responding to instruction, communicating, imitating, and turn taking. One of the social coaching methods that we use teaches children how to play appropriately with toys. Many children with ASD initially play repetitively with toys, mouthing them, banging them, or spinning them. Starting with a simple cause-and-effect toy that the child has shown to prefer, the trainer says, "Do this" while performing appropriate action with the toy. Immediately the toy is handed to the child and he is reinforced for correct action; if incorrect, he is prompted to help him get it right.

Toys are also used as motivators to teach the skill of taking turns. This sequence is begun with a highly preferred toy. The child plays with the toy for a bit, and then the adult says, "My turn," places a hand gently on the child's hand, and helps her release her grasp. The adult keeps the toy for just a second and hands it back, saying, "My turn" again as a prompt for the child to repeat. This game is continued, slowly increasing the time the toy is taken. The child soon learns that she will get her toy back and begins to tolerate sharing and turn taking.

The gentle, consistent approach of the Star Program, based on American Behavioral Analysis (ABA) strategies, helps some children begin to listen, look, and follow simple direction. This behavioral work helps set the foundation for participating with others, an important component of game playing.

Pivotal Response Training is another aspect of behavioral strategy that utilizes a *pivotal* moment during a play session in which the potential for communication can occur. For example, if a child is enjoying being bounced, he is given many moments to enjoy this, and then the movement is stopped. The adult then looks expectantly at the child and provides a clear verbal model, "Bounce? More?" or "I want bounce?" If the child makes a sound, eye contact, approximates the words, or says the words, the bouncing immediately begins again. If there is no response, a moment or two passes and the adult models the word "Bounce!" and begins again.

Example of Pivotal Response Training

Ronnie was the new kid at Social Club. I thought I'd win him over right away with the day's plans because it started off with blowing through a straw and turning a bowl of water mixed with soap into a mountain of bubbles. Playing with sponges at the water table followed this. Kids tend to love water play.

Reggie took one look at the water activities and started crying and clinging to his aide, Yoli. "He hates water," Yoli explained. "We have a hard time getting him to wash his hands."

Well, I thought maybe, for now, we could get him interested in the other planned game, which was Hit the Homemade Piñata with a bat. (We call it homemade because our piñata is nothing more than a plastic bag stuffed with newspaper.) Reggie refused to leave the security of Yoli's lap to walk the five feet to where the piñata hung.

I brought the plastic bat over to him, grabbed someone's keychain, and dangled the keys enticingly over his head. He was tempted enough to allow Yoli to do a hand-over-hand technique and bat at the keys. When they jangled after being hit, he was willing to do it again a few times. I expanded the repertoire by having him hit an empty water bottle instead. When he hit the bottle and it went flying, he laughed. The next time he laughed louder. Ah, I thought, now I've got him. For the following turns, I used the Pivotal Response to get him to communicate his desire to repeat the experience. I held the bottle up and asked, "More?" First I got a nondescript sound. The next time I got eye contact, and then the word approximation, "Mo." Each response was rewarded with another chance to knock the bottle out of my hand.

With a quick movement, we transferred him to the piñata site and he happily whacked away at that for quite a while. Not willing to let go of the water plan, I brought him a large, sopping-wet sponge and squeezed it on the ground near his feet.

Because of his improved mood; along with his growing sense that maybe we might be okay, he took the sponge and squeezed it too. I filled it back up with water, and we took turns squeezing and dripping and dripping and squeezing until it was time to return to class.

Picture Exchange Communication (PEC) can be used with children who are delayed in their speech. Once hearing or oral motor problems are ruled out or addressed, children are shown how to use pictures as a way of communicating and to begin to use simple sentences, such as "I want airplane," to express their needs. Picture schedules are also used to help children understand the sequence of activities in their day. Seeing what comes next helps eliminate the anxiousness often associated with transitions from one activity to another.

Playing on the floor with the child many times during the day provides important opportunities for him to learn and practice receptive and expressive language, and to have fun doing something that really interests him.

Floortime, which was named and modeled by Dr. Stanley Greenspan, lets the child initiate the activity, and then the adult expands and improvises on the game to make it a moment of shared attention where they are both focusing and relating about the same object or activity. Improvisational play, especially during Floortime, provides other opportunities for the child to experience back-and-forth play and creative thinking. Dr. Greenspan's work has shown that engaging a child by starting with her interest, then challenging and expanding that interest, increases synaptic connection and promotes healthy mental development. Greenspan's research shows that the effect of joy and the experience of engaged fun are crucial in developing the brain.

Along with concurrent therapies, diet should also be considered. According to the Autism Network for Dietary Intervention, current research shows that many cases of autism may result from an immune-system dysfunction that affects the body's ability to break down certain proteins and to combat yeasts and bacteria. A gluten-free, casein-free (GFCF) diet can improve the symptoms in children whose behaviors are being caused by the abnormal breakdown of these proteins. Gluten and gluten-like proteins are found in wheat and other grains, including oats, rye, barley, bulgur, durum, kamut, and spelt, and foods made from those grains. Casein is a protein found in milk and foods containing milk, such as cheese, butter, yogurt, ice cream, whey, and even some brands of margarine. A change in diet will not work for every child, but a significant number do respond, sometimes remarkably.

Numerous studies also show that certain synthetic food additives can have serious learning, behavior, and health effects for sensitive people. Methods such as the Feingold Diet eliminate these additives from the diet: artificial coloring, artificial flavoring, aspartame (Nutrasweet, an artificial sweetener) and the preservatives BHA, BHT, and TBHQ.

To learn more specifics about a variety of helpful intervention programs, such as Applied Behavior Analysis, Star Program, Floortime, Picture Exchange Communication, the Miller Method, Pivotal Response Training, the Feingold Diet, and others, please see the Web sites listed in Appendix II.

How the Games Address Specific Characteristics of Children with ASD and SPD

Many children on the autism spectrum and with Sensory Processing Disorders may be overwhelmed or anxious and use defensiveness as a way of protecting themselves. A social situation that we may see as normal can have stressful components for them, such as not knowing what will happen next or what is expected of them. Any irritating sounds, smells, textures, uncomfortable lighting, or loud noises can put their systems on high alert. They live in a state of perpetual fear. In this state, they are easily distracted and unable to stay focused or to calm themselves. It is imperative to figure out what is stressing them and address it.

First, it's important to provide structure. The room should be uncluttered, with soft, natural lighting. Providing a picture schedule that visually shows what will be happening next can reduce anxiousness. The sessions should be familiar and predictable. For example, always start and end with the same songs, or start each game session with the same obstacle course game before introducing variations.

To reduce children's anxiety during an activity, tell or show them what is expected of them and when it's going to end, for example, "You have two things to do. Write on the paper with this candle and then paint over the wax." Or you might draw a small schedule of the activity. For example, draw a picture of writing with a candle, followed by a picture of painting with a brush, and then the word "DONE," or a picture of the child's favorite toy or activity that he can have or do once the work is done.

Along with providing structure, allow some time for free play and checking things out. Although you should keep most of the game materials out of sight to decrease distraction, put some select ones on the shelves to encourage exploration, or set aside a time when children can sit on the rug or lie on soft blankets and play with a variety of toys that they choose from a toy box. Free playtime, perhaps with soft music, should be designed to be a calming period before or after structured games to reduce any stress that they may be feeling.

Other calming activities in the games include:

Wrapping the child up in a blanket or large soft fabric
Applying bandage wraps to arms or legs (playing mummy)
Wearing weighted items, such as vests, lap blankets, shoulder beanbags, plush animals, and wrist or ankle weights
Gently massaging extremities or back with lotion
Slow back-and-forth motion, such as swinging, rocking, or gliding

Aquatic therapy is a wonderful way to work with children with ASD or SPD. The games in this book include some you can do in shallow water, with a water table or kiddie pool, and others that can be done in deeper water, such as a pool or lake, always with adult supervision. As with the other games, keep to a predictable schedule, while including the occasional new games for variety. Also allow for some time when the children can initiate an activity. In addition to the specific games, give the children free moments in the water when they can play quietly alone or with another under adult supervision. To keep everyone safe and to account for distractibility, always have each child paired with an adult while in the water.

Calming games include massaging, swinging, rocking, squishing, and other deep-pressure activities.

DIFFERENT INTERESTS

Children on the autism spectrum can have different interests from typical kids, such as lining up objects according to size or repeatedly spinning a top—interests that typically revolve around inanimate objects and not people. Although it's fine for kids to have their preferences, there are many kids on the autism spectrum who would never participate in social activities if given the choice. If we want these children to enjoy socializing, they need to develop the willingness to participate. Because we don't want to cause undue stress in a child, we must find a balance and a compromise.

Provide enough variety so that activities preferred by the children are included and new ones can be explored in order to expand their interests and make them more social. For example, lining things up according to size or color is a calming activity for many kids with ASD. In an expanded and social game, use paint samples from the hardware store that have a variety of hues. Have another child hand a sample to the player and have him find the matching color. The variety of hues expands their matching and sorting skills and honors their need to put their world in a predictable order. Another child's handing him the colors or taking a turn to match adds the social element.

If a child wants to repeat an activity, such as jumping off the side of the pool many times, give her extra time to do this—unless you think that the child is persevering on this activity as a way to avoid other activities or people. If this is the case, then give jumping as a reward for trying another activity in which she is less interested.

Give children opportunities to take the lead. For example, play games in which one child performs a movement and the action is "Can you do what I do?" imitated by everyone. If Manny is kicking and splashing his feet, we all do it too.

DIFFICULTY WITH TURN TAKING

Turn taking can be a difficult concept. Children often have a hard time giving up a toy. They may feel like they won't be able to get it back and they see no value or purpose for the interaction. Work on "my turn, your turn," in which the child plays with a preferred toy for a bit; then the adult says, "My turn" and gestures for the toy or helps the child pass it to her, keeping it only for a short time before returning it and saying, "Jenna's turn."

Waiting for one's turn in games that require only one person to go at a time is another challenge. There is often an inability to delay gratification. Many typical preschoolers also have trouble with this and get excited about having their turn and frequently "cut" in line. Not uncommon also is the unawareness that others are having a turn. One strategy is to allow or encourage a child to jump in place while waiting his turn. Often an adult standing behind the waiting child and compressing his shoulder is effective. Also, start with a shorter waiting time so that gratification comes quickly, and then gradually increase the waiting time. Singing a song or chant that goes with the game also is effective.

Because many of the kids are primarily visual learners, instead of using verbal cues, you might use something concrete, such as an egg timer or a handheld manipulative, such as a token to indicate whose turn it is. In the "pass the token" method, a token is given to the child whose turn it is and passed to the next child when the turn is finished. When they get the token, they know it's their turn. If a child jumps ahead of the line, gently remind him by asking, "Do you have the token? When you get it, then it's your turn."

Another strategy is to help the child pay attention to the child before him. You could say something like, "This is John. Wait for John to have his turn. You go right after him."

Equally possible is that a child will wander off instead of waiting for her turn. Such words as "Don't miss your turn! Your turn is soon!" while redirecting her back can help, or try physically jumping the child up and down so that she is active while waiting.

Sitting snugly and comfortably on an adult's lap also works for kids who have a tendency to jump up and grab and who need help to stay seated and wait.

The Sponge Pass is an example of a turn-taking game in the water in which each child gets a chance to dip and squeeze a sponge before passing it on. When we need to shorten the wait we sometimes use two sponges so the wait is not as long and everyone has more turns.

MELTDOWNS

Frustration can result from an inability to communicate or verbally express needs; an overload of stress, especially if bottled up for a while, can result in unexpected outbursts. Though each child is different, there are some commonalities that cause stress. Environmental factors can affect the children's sensory systems and they are often unable to tune out information, including irritating noises; unpleasant smells; and uncomfortable textures and sights, such as flickering lights. Not knowing what lies ahead can also be very stressful to a child, as many children have difficulty with transitions and changes in activities.

It's important to give calming input frequently in recurring doses, rather than waiting until the child becomes upset. Following a jumping game with a deep-pressure wrapping game or a lotion massage provides a calming transition period between activities.

Again, the schedule should be consistent and generally predictable: first a greeting circle and then the obstacle course, and so on. To help children handle change, after you do the predictable sequence of activity, introduce a variation on a game that they have already tried. For example, one day the children are crawling through a tunnel made by people's legs, the next time they are crawling through a tunnel made from an opened box.

For children who need more preparation for change, have photos of the games you will play so they can take turns choosing which game is played next. Also, help model behavior to avoid meltdowns due to frustration. For example, you might demonstrate not being able to get the large cylinder in a hole that is too small and say such words as "Uh-oh! I will do this a different way. This way is not working," and demonstrate finding a different way without getting upset.

By being alert to possible stresses, you can avoid meltdowns before they occur. For some children, this can mean having time alone with only one adult, such as by taking a short walk away from the group.

Also encourage children to say what they need if they can or by imitating words. "I want walk" can be taught to mean the child needs a break from the activity. To prevent the child using this cue as a way to always avoid activities, the response can be, "First throw the ball and next we walk."

In aquatic therapy, you should be particularly aware of the environmental factors. Is the water temperature warm enough? Does the child need more shade or more sun? Is the child tired, and does he need to float on his back for a while rather than join in the splashing game? Or did the splashing game scare him, and does he need a gentler version? Is she starting to feel confined being in the circle, and does she need a moment to move vigorously?

DIFFICULTIES WITH TRANSITIONS

Children with autism can have difficulty with transitions or sudden changes. Some children have a hard time transitioning from one activity to another or from a familiar adult to an unfamiliar one. Predictable situations are comforting but because changes in life are inevitable, it is important to help the children deal with them. A predictable structure brings comfort, and so does the awareness that one can handle change.

As previously stated, using a picture schedule lets children know what is coming next. And consistency in the schedule means the games always begin and end in the same fashion. You can also give ample warning about what's coming up. For example, let them know that after the obstacle course, you're going to play the blanket game. Or when giving free time, use a timer so the children know that when the buzzer rings, free time ends and a structured activity begins.

Often, you can reduce the children's resistance to change by making sure the children know that they will return to a preferred activity. For example, if a child loves jumping, you could say, "We are going to do some painting now but when we are done you can jump some more." This way the child feels more in control and knows that it's OK to stop because the activity will be resumed later. Sometimes holding on to a preferred object while switching activities can add the consistency that is needed to help them make the transition.

Besides a predictable routine, specific games can help children deal with change. For example, in the game One, Two, Three—Change, children in inner tubes are purposely interchanged by the adults in order to develop this skill.

AVOIDING EYE CONTACT

It is often difficult for children on the spectrum to look and listen at the same time. It is too much sensory information to take in at one time and can be extremely threatening. The noted pediatrician T. Berry Brazelton, MD explains this phenomenon in his book *Touchpoints:* "A hypersensitive baby can be approached through one modality at a time—either speaking softly or looking in her face or rocking her gently—but only one. As she begins to assimilate each modality and to respond warily, another modality can gradually be added until finally all three are together and she is able to respond to them" (p. 75).

Don't insist on eye contact, but do praise it and encourage it. If a child looks at you when you are talking to him, you might say, "I like that you looked at me" or "It feels nice when you look at me."

Encourage "shared attention," where the child looks at the object or activity on which everyone is focused. The praise in that situation might sound like this: "I liked the way you looked at the box while you were throwing the ball." In this way you are stating what the child did without subjective judgment. Instead of saying a generic "Good job" or "Strong work," you are describing what you see. When a nonverbal child is enjoying the moment, you might stop the activity and then respond to the child's eye contact as a request for more by restarting the desired activity and modeling the word or sign "More!"

You should also be sensitive to the cultural aspects of eye contact. In many cultures, such as Asian, direct eye contact from a child to an adult is not as encouraged as it is in European or American cultures.

You are more likely to get spontaneous and even prolonged eye contact during hydrotherapy, when the body is already softly rocking in the water's current. From that calmer place children are often better able to take in and integrate the barrage of visual information. Do calming games in the water, such as holding a child so she can float on her back with her head resting on an adult's shoulder. In that calm state, add sound, such as soft crooning. Do some high-energy games as well, such as jumping over little waves in the ocean. The enjoyment of the movements and the excitement of anticipation can put the child in a joyful, accepting mode in which she is willing to seek out more input.

FOLLOWING VERBAL INSTRUCTIONS

Children on the autism spectrum can find it difficult to follow verbal instructions, as they are unlikely to ask you to repeat or clarify what was said. This may result in the child's following part of your instructions or doing nothing at all. The child is not being disobedient, but more likely didn't understand what to do. These children may also have significant auditory processing problems or may be selectively choosing what they listen to.

For these children, keep the instructions short and give them one at a time. Instead of instructing the children to "Cut the paper and glue it to the board," say, "Cut the paper here." After the paper is cut, say, "Put glue on the paper," and so forth. You might also have an example of the finished product to view or a picture aid. As children get more able and more familiar with tasks, more than one step may be given at a time. Children who are verbal can be asked to state or repeat the steps of the tasks before they begin.

To help the children who are more visual, you can give picture cues of the components of the task and the finished product. However, it's important to note that not all children with autism need visuals. As Stephen Shore, an adult with autism and author of *Understanding Autism for Dummies*, said, "There is a myth that all persons with autism have visually based learning styles. . . . While most people with autism are visually based not all of us are. Therefore, it's important to be sensitive to the possibility that a person with autism may favor the kinesthetic, aural, or other modality for learning. What can be said is that whatever the learning style is it will probably be to an extreme."

Aquatic therapy instructions are generally only one- or two-step processes. They are often sung and repeated in song because it is often easier to listen to singing than to talking. Singing employs rhythm, which can also be very calming. For example, in Fill the Bucket in which children need to fill their cups and pour the water into a bucket until it's full, sing the following to the tune of "Skip to My Lou":

> Fill your cup and fill the bucket
> Fill your cup and fill the bucket,

Fill your cup and fill the bucket,

All the way to the top

The words in the song are timed to the action. In this way children hear the instructions many times and can visually see when the task is done.

SOCIAL AWARENESS

The child on the autism spectrum may be eager to join in group spontaneous play, but will instead stand on the sidelines, occupying himself and ignoring everyone around him. The social world can be a mystery to children on the autism spectrum. We all tend to shy away from situations in which we feel uncomfortable, but kids on the autism spectrum especially need a lot of encouragement and assistance in social interactions. Most don't know how to initiate contact and, because they typically don't give eye contact, they may fail to notice what is going on or how to imitate an appropriate action in order to be included.

To encourage socializing, there are games that allow children to do activities that need others. For example, in Blanket Ride, one or two children are placed on a blanket and others have to pull on the blanket to give them a ride. Or the Bubble Blowing game, in which children blow through their straws into a communal container and make a glorious mountain of bubbles emerge.

If more proprioceptive feedback is needed in order for children to be aware of playing with others, try such games as A Kid Sandwich or Rolling Children. In these games, children are physically rolled over each other or are squeezed together to increase the physical awareness of others.

In fine motor games, if a child needs glue, for example, encourage him to ask another child to pass it to him rather than have an adult do it. Or have two children take turns accomplishing a task, such as putting all the cut-up straws back into a container.

You may also want to pair up a child on the spectrum with a friend, relative, or classmate who will be a good social influence. This child might be one who is patient or one who is a bit bossy and will be more insistent on interaction. Who the chosen playmate is will depend on what the child needs.

In aquatic therapy, because it's fun to play with and in water, this joyful state of mind makes it easier to be open to relating. The repeated reciprocal and group interaction games encourage children to try ways to be part of the group. For example, in the game in which everyone fills their small cups and dumps the water into a big bucket, something fun happens for everyone when the bucket is full. In another game, all the children get the chance to squirt water on the adults and each other.

If you play the same games consistently, the familiarity of the games also makes it easier to participate.

MOTOR SKILLS

Motor skills can be a big problem for kids on the spectrum. Gross motor activities requiring coordination, such as various types of sports, or even simple tasks, such as jumping forward, can be difficult for a child with autism. There are always exceptions to this, and there are some children on the spectrum that have excellent balance and motor planning skills. These are usually the ones who can climb up precarious heights and perch on small areas with no difficulty.

Fine motor skills can also be challenging to those on the autism spectrum. Using zippers or buttons, closing and opening items, writing, and other tasks requiring detailed motor coordination may not be within the child's capability. As with any feelings of incompetence, gentle encouragement helps best.

When doing games that require fine motor activities, help the child feel successful by starting the action and allowing the child to complete it. For example, loosen the wrapper on a straw but let the child take it off. As much as possible, encourage independence in play as in self-care. Or you might do a hand-over-hand technique when doing a new task, such as painting, so they can feel the motion that is needed.

During gross motor skills games, start from where children can be successful. For example, begin to teach eye-hand coordination with targets that are close and easy to hit, and then slowly increase the challenge. Also keep the games short to avoid frustration and keep them fun!

To increase motor control, play games that require changing directions or "stop" and "go" movements.

Moving in water is moving against resistance, which increases muscle strength. In this way, all activities in the water increase physical strength, an important underlying component of coordination. You can't throw a ball well if you don't have the strength to throw it far. The water also provides a haven that supports balance and equilibrium. It helps the child to move in a more controlled and fluid manner, and there is less likelihood that children will trip, stumble, and fall.

ATTENTIVENESS

On the one hand, children on the autism spectrum often have poor attending skills. On the other hand, they can seem to notice everything. They may also exhibit "selective attention," purposely ignoring what they don't want to hear and noticing what they do. They may not hear you calling them to wash up for dinner, but they do hear the crinkled paper of the candy being unwrapped in the next room. They might be hearing everything, even if they appear to be staring out the window or avoiding your gaze and not responding.

Paying attention takes energy. Sometimes much of that energy is consumed by filtering out excess stimulation around them, and children are not able to attend to what you are presenting. Also, if the activity is one they're not interested in, they often have a very short attention span. They might concentrate only for a few minutes and then require a break or a schedule to get back on track.

If a child is not attending to a task, you could make the object of the game more visible, such as by colorfully decorating a box into which they are to throw balls. The person giving the instruction might wear a zany hat in order to be noticed.

Massaging can be effective prior to an activity by increasing awareness and helping the brain and body to self-organize. For example, when the children are sitting in a circle before rolling the ball to each other, use deep-pressure massage while singing such words as "This is the way we squeeze your arms, squeeze your arms, squeeze your arms. This is way we squeeze your arms so early in the morning," and so on for different body parts. Don't forget to give gentle pressure to hands and soles of feet as well.

If children are distracted during play, you might physically jump them up and down, quickly massage and squeeze their muscles, or give a firm hug to bring them back to the present moment. A firm downward pressure on shoulders often keeps a child alert and present, especially helpful when waiting for a turn. Try to be aware of offending sensory stimuli, and limit any that might be distracting.

Before group games in the "hot tub" during which the children are required to sit and attend for a prolonged period, massaging can help get them ready for social play.

Physical action also helps children to attend. Swirling around in the water can bring a child's attention delightfully back to the activity at hand and away from his private world where socializing is difficult.

ANXIOUSNESS

Some children on the spectrum are calm in their own world but anxious, overactive, or uncomfortably sensitive when aware of the rest of the world. Their brains misinterpret sensory input and go into a protective fight, flight, or fright mode even though there is no "real" danger. In this state, the child may hit, bite, or yell (fight); run away or become hyperactive (flight); or shut down and appear spaced out or have a glazed internal look (fright). When made to interact, the child may get clingy, tearful, or panicked, or perseverate in an activity, such as flapping her hand to self-regulate and self-calm.

Such activities as running, jumping, bouncing, lifting, and pushing, and other movements that use the large muscles of the body, can help children stay calm by stimulating the cerebellum, which releases calming hormones. Wearing a weighted vest or carrying a weighted stuffed animal has the dual purpose of calming and giving continual feedback so the children can stay present. A picture schedule with pictures of the activities that will be presented can also be helpful to reduce anxieties about the unknown.

Allowing children to hold on to a preferred toy or object during a game can reduce fear. Being given a toy as a reward after each game can put the emphasis on pleasurable anticipation. Their experience of having had fun the last time they did the activities also contributes to their ability to stay calm. The consistent structure makes them feel safe, and the fun of the activities rewards them for staying present.

As stated previously, it's useful to notice what happened before the child showed signs of anxiousness. Look for possible sensory causes, such as sudden movement, excess noise, and overreaction to an unstable surface or certain smells.

Water provides a consistent gentle, comforting pressure, and the buoyancy provides a repetitive and rhythmical movement, which is calming. Being held in the arms of an adult or in the security of a small inner tube can also provide comfort. The freedom to move independently in a foam padded suit also comforts.

COMMUNICATION SKILLS

Most of the children with ASD or SPD need help in communicating and can present with nonfunctional language skills. They are typically delayed in language acquisition and resort to younger forms of communication, such as crying, screaming, hitting, and biting. They can be echolalic and perseverative as well.

Giving children the methods to express their needs through sign language, words, PECs (picture exchange cards), or other augmentative communication is essential to support their individual strengths and help decrease their frustration.

It can help to describe what the child is doing and thinking as a "voice over" to give him the vocabulary for what he is doing and to help him learn the meaningful words in a situation. You can also encourage children to respond using the Pivotal Response Training model. For example, when the child is fully engaged in an activity, pause the activity so that the child will request more. Depending on the child's skill level, a gesture, an approximation, a word, or a sentence are encouraged, and the child can see that by giving a response, she will get what she wants. This shows the child that communicating works.

Games that involve pointing an index finger can also be helpful because pointing is a way of attracting shared attention.

There is a lot of singing and chanting used in the water games. Children who don't have the words to say what they want may sing the tune. For example, a child might start to sing the tune of a song we've made up, "Going to the Pool," to let us know she is ready to go there.

There are also many moments during the water games when a form of communication is needed in order to continue the games. For example, the child must place her hand in an open palm gesture or say the word "Please" before receiving a wanted water toy.

INDEPENDENCE

Children with ASD or SPD can have difficulty being independent for a variety of reasons. They might not have the fine motor skills to accomplish the tasks they need to do to take care of their needs. They might be feeling too anxious to be on their own. Or they might not understand what is needed to achieve independence in the situation.

When children need things, suggest that they ask a peer so that they can begin to see that they can get help, information, and companionship from others. Offer options between games on occasion—"Do you want to play the jumping game or the throwing game?"—so children can see that there are choices when making decisions.

You can use prompts, either visual or physical, to help children understand what to do next. These prompts can then be faded out over time. Fine motor games can be used to work on activities of daily living, such as buttoning, zipping, and snapping.

There are opportunities to teach children self-help skills as they change in and out of their swim clothes. Encourage independence by teaching them how to do things for themselves. When teaching children to dress themselves, do the first steps and let them finish the rest so that they are part of the process; eventually, step by step, they can learn it all. And try different modifications.

If tying shoes independently seems too difficult to tackle now, start with shoes with Velcro closures.

MALADAPTIVE BEHAVIORS

As Jene Aviram of Natural Learning Concepts points out on her exceptionally autistic-friendly Web site (www.nlconcepts.com), children on the autism spectrum often exhibit behaviors that we don't understand.

> He might flick his fingers through the air, make a fist and bang his knee. And do it again and again. Or, he makes a strange noise every time he stands up. The child does not do these behaviors to be disruptive, but simply because he feels a need to do them. Compare it to the compelling behavior many of us have of biting one's nails, twirling one's hair, or cracking one's knuckles. While we might be confused by their behavior, they are often equally confused by our rules and expectations. Children on the autism spectrum are unique and they all have different behaviors.

> Children also might use the same odd behavior for different reasons. Hand flapping, for example, can give a hyposensitive child the stimulation he needs to increase his alertness and wake up his nervous system. Conversely, a hypersensitive child may flap his hands to block out the external environment, decrease tension, or release pleasurable endorphins in the body.

Children with ASD might stand apart from other kids but, just like everyone else, they want to be loved and accepted for who they are. Try to understand what need is being met by the child's behavior. Consider what activity just preceded it. This helps us to develop a sensory diet to apply intervention techniques preceding the behavior or in therapeutic doses throughout the day. For example, does it appear that Noah started flapping his hand right after a group of children walked into the room? If flapping is a way to self-calm, you can help the child find other, more socially acceptable ways to self-calm, such as spinning tops or twiddling with a necklace. Or you may need to target other sensory systems, such as the vestibular or proprioceptive, to help keep the child's nervous system in a calm but alert state. At the same time, you want the child to understand that if flapping is what he needs, it's okay to flap sometimes! (When he's able to understand, bring in the concept of self-advocacy. It's socially helpful for him to know that flapping in private, such as in the bathroom, can avoid odd looks from others.)

Learning to initiate and sustain social interaction is a complex skill that develops over time and affects, eventually, one's ability to function in a class-room, hold a job, form satisfying relationships, develop confidence, and be able to explain one's sensory needs. These skills are the building blocks that are laid through early intervention games.

How the Games Address Sensory Processing Challenges

When children are exposed to a variety of playful situations, they will begin to take risks and do things they might normally avoid. Also, exposing children to multiple sensory experiences helps new sensations become more familiar. As their need to avoid or seek out extra stimulation decreases, their emotional energy is freed up so that more is available for socializing. Therapy as play is designed to stimulate and challenge the senses and the social needs. The games focus on the varying difficulties the children have and address those issues in a variety of ways.

The games use the "just right" challenge. Using observation and experience, you can use the games to give children just the right amount of challenge to motivate them and stimulate changes in the way their systems process sensory information, but not so much as to make them shut down or go into sensory overload. For example, a child who is tactile defensive will often tolerate a deep pressured touch. As his system becomes more comfortable with touch, he becomes increasingly open to accepting lighter touch and to experimenting with touching.

Because each child is unique, each game can be modified to suit individual children. Modifications are described at the end of every game.

TACTILE DEFENSIVENESS

Children who are hypersensitive to touch will avoid being hugged, touching messy materials, and eating certain foods. They may toe walk to avoid touching the floor or use negative behavior to get out of having their hair brushed or washed. In more extreme cases, they may even resort to self-injurious behaviors. And they may find being close to other children threatening.

This defensiveness can also affect learning skills that require a hand-over-hand approach. For example, placing a hand over a child's to help her learn how to draw a circle or catch a ball facilitates learning through muscle memory. If a child pulls her hand away from such an approach, you need to find other methods to help her learn and to help her tolerate touch.

Start by approaching the child slowly and from the front, positioning yourself on the same level as the child and allowing her additional personal space if needed. You can also allow time for the child to pace the room or move freely during activities. If boundaries are required, you can use positioning tools, such as colored spots, taped boxes, and chalk lines.

Use fine motor activities that give children the opportunity to play with various textures, such as finger painting with puddings and whipped topping; filling and dumping out a container of rice, pinto beans, or popcorn; tracing in flour, sugar, and bird seed; and playing with vibrating toys. These kinds of activities help children to become capable of adjusting to sensory input through repetition and continuous exposure. If a child at first needs gloves, "finger mittens," or a stick to touch some kinds of materials, go ahead and let her use them. Then gradually encourage the child to use bare hands. Unless the child insists on washing, try to gradually lengthen the amount of time between touching something and washing it off.

Walking in the warm sand of the beach; playing in dry and wet sand; and having parts of the body, such as their feet, buried in sand provide an interesting challenge and also help children enlarge their tolerance. A sustained, consistent surrounding pressure is calming to the nervous system and can help to decrease overall defensiveness. Being close to a body of water allows children to wash off when overloaded and then try again. Activities should be paced according to the child's tolerance, such as starting with burying only toes in the sand and then rinsing the toes in a nearby bucket of water.

BODY AWARENESS AND COORDINATION

The proprioceptive system receives sensations from joints, muscles, and connective tissues that tell us what our bodies are doing. Children who are weak in this sensory area are likely to bump into others or things and have difficulty staying in line or navigating within a crowd. They don't have a clear sense of their bodies in space and how they relate to other people and objects because they aren't adequately processing the feedback from their proprioceptive systems.

Giving them "heavy work" activities provides additional muscle work and joint input, which exaggerates feedback to the brain to increase body awareness. There are many games that provide proprioceptive input through lifting, pushing, and pulling heavy objects, and by engaging in activities that compress (push together) or distract (pull apart) the joints. Such games as getting wrapped in cloth to make a "sushi," getting squeezed together to make a "sandwich," pulling others along on a blanket, jumping on the trampoline, or playing Tug-of-War can provide children with the extra stimulation needed to stay alert and aware of their bodies. Games that involve swinging and rocking help children organize their body awareness and are also calming. Obstacle courses provide lots of opportunity to go over, under, in between, and around different surfaces, including some that are moveable. Massaging, brushing, firm holds, and loving squeezes all also add to body awareness.

The resistance of water provides a continual sense of awareness of body movements. Specific games, such as jumping and landing in the water, pushing against tubes, being pulled along in a train, dragging boogie boards through water, being passed from adult to adult, and being squeezed when playing London Bridge, are only some of the many games in which children become aware of their bodies in the water.

BALANCE ISSUES

The vestibular system gives us the sense of movement and lets us know when we are off center. Children who are less aware of this input have problems with balance and are likely to fall more easily, be clumsy, or have poor coordination. Some of these children are said to have "gravitational insecurity" and may get upset or even frightened when walking on uneven surfaces or at any time their balance is challenged.

These children benefit from the vestibular input that can be obtained by spinning and swinging and, to a lesser extent, any type of movement. Again, as in the therapy for proprioceptive awareness, exaggeration and repetition increase the possibility for attentiveness.

Such games as spinning in a saucer, being swung like a hammock, swinging on swings, or being spun around in carts with wheels all stimulate the vestibular system and make children more aware of their centers. Children with balance issues may also be very cautious or scared and avoid roughhousing, tending to prefer quiet sitting while others play. For these children, start movements slowly and gradually increase the tempo. Rather than swinging, for example, have these children start off pushing someone else before being pushed themselves. Getting rides on blankets and in boxes also help incorporate balance in a safe way. Walking backward and running games also require concentration in order to keep one's balance.

As part of an obstacle course, children can learn to walk on a low balance beam forward, sideways, and backward. The course can also challenge and increase a child's balancing skills through activities that require balancing on one foot while kicking or hopping, walking across the uneven surface of a trampoline, and tiptoeing along a line.

Games that integrate other senses, such as jumping and simultaneously throwing a ball at a target, are useful for children who are ready for a higher level of sensory integration.

Getting spun around while in an inner tube, being tossed in the air, jumping off the side of the pool, twirling in the water, and feeling the wave action of the water are all ways children get vestibular input in the water.

When playing on the beach, children have to adjust their balance to stay upright on the uneven surfaces of the sand.

VISUAL DISTRACTION

Some children are visually distractible and have difficulty knowing where to put their attention. They may not be able to distinguish the dominant figure from the background of stimuli, other sights may easily distract them, or they may not respond easily to visual stimulation because they can't tolerate the glare from the sunlight or the flickering from fluorescent lights.

Simplifying the environment and reducing visual clutter can have a calming effect on these children. For example, play on solid-colored rugs instead of patterned ones and keep only a few toys in view.

For the child who seems visually "tuned out," and who has trouble getting aroused for play, you might add more noticeable details, such as a brightly decorated box for a throwing game and colored rice for a fine motor game. If playing an imitation game, such as a modified "Simon Says," "Simon" might wear a fanciful hat to call attention to himself as the one to imitate.

Because verbal instructions may require too much concentration and get tuned out, use picture cues. For example, in the can bowling game, it can be easier to understand what is expected if two pictures are shown: one of the cans in a tower formation and then another of a ball knocking them down. Children can see what is expected.

The blue color of a pool, the ocean, or a lake naturally provides a stimulating as well as a calming background for water games. Using colorful tubes for a target in a throwing game or decorating Ping-Pong balls for a scooping game add attractive and interesting visual stimulation that help draw a child's attention.

AUDITORY SENSITIVITIES

Some children are very sensitive to sounds, tones, and frequencies, and will even cover their ears when they hear people singing. Certain sounds and volumes can be intolerable. Some children find it difficult to pay attention to both their visual and hearing systems; they can't give eye contact and listen at the same time. Often children with hearing sensitivities are delayed in their speech because they have blocked out many sounds or may not be processing them properly.

For many of these children, hearing instruction in song is an easier way to listen and it helps calm and organize auditory input. The volume of the song can be adjusted to fit the tolerance of the children. Sing or chant the words to the activities they are doing. "Throw the balls into the box, into the box, into the box. Throw the balls into the box. Where did the balls go?"

Children can also experiment with playing a keyboard or making music with other instruments.

If normal sounds are a problem, you can try earplugs, earmuffs, or quiet time-outs with headphones.

Being out in nature and listening to the birds or going to the beach and hearing the waves are gentle ways to encourage listening. Waves and other outdoor sounds can sometimes provide that "white noise" that many of these kids find so calming and soothing. Often children with ASD like the hum of the fan, the air conditioning, the dryer, the vacuum, and so on because of that constant low pitch. To decrease sensitivities, louder noises should be gently approached.

OLFACTORY SENSITIVITIES

About 70 to 75 percent of what we perceive as taste actually comes from our sense of smell. Taste buds allow us to perceive only bitter, salty, sweet, and sour flavors. It's the odor molecules from food that give us most of our taste sensation. Children with strong sensitivities to smells might also have eating issues and would benefit from a professional evaluation.

For some children with sensory issues, certain odors can stimulate them, calm them, or send them into sensory overload. Some children want to smell everything in order to stimulate their olfactory sense. Because smells give us so much information, children who are not getting enough feedback in this area seek more.

Scents can be either soothing or stimulating. Although everyone has different preferences, vanilla and rose are generally calming, whereas peppermint and citrus are usually stimulating. Play games of identifying smells or simply expose children to a variety of smells, such as maple syrup, apple, peanut butter, and soap.

Now that you have a sense of what to look for and an understanding of the underlying reasons for what you see, it's time to play. Your attitude affects the ambience, so enjoy yourself, play right along with the kids, and take the time to adore them, even when they aren't being adorable. We are all doing our best and we can all learn to get better. Meanwhile . . . let the games begin!

CHAPTER 3

Social Gross Motor Games

A Kid Sandwich

Guaranteed to bring giggles, this game is especially liked by children with ASD because it stimulates the proprioceptive system and has the delight of a group hug.

GOALS

Awareness of others
Pretend play
Following directions
Imagination
Modulation
Tolerating physical closeness
Matching pictures

MATERIALS

Optional:
Pictures of sandwiches

Picture of a boy eating a sandwich

Pictures of sandwich ingredients, such as pickles, cheese, lettuce, and
    so on

Masking tape or footprints for the floor

SETUP

Have the children stand in a circle with the adults. Tell the children they are
going to make a sandwich. Two children will be the bread. Other children
will be the ingredients, and some will be the eaters of the sandwich.

DIRECTIONS

Pick one child to stand in the center of the circle and be the bread. Then ask,
"What else shall we put in this sandwich?" If the children at first don't come
up with ideas, suggest some. For example, say, "Let's add some cheese" and
then pick another child to be the cheese. Put that child directly in front of
the child who is the piece of bread. Continue naming and choosing children
to be the ingredients, such as ham, pickles, tomato, lettuce, and so on, each
time placing the child in front of the last ingredient. End with another piece
of bread. You may also find that some children might call out an ingredient
that isn't usually in a sandwich, such as rice or chocolate. Go ahead and put
whatever they say in the sandwich!

After the sandwich is made, gently squeeze all the ingredients together
and announce, "It's time to eat." Everyone who is not part of the sandwich
pretends to eat, smacking their lips and making chewing sounds. Yum!
Then, start all over and make a new sandwich!

WHAT IS BEING LEARNED

♦ Because the ingredients all get squished together, this game provides
the proprioceptive feedback that children with ASD often crave, as well
as the friendliness and warmth of connecting with another human in
a nonthreatening and silly way. Besides experimenting with a fun way
to play with and get next to each other, children are playing pretend, an

important skill. Everyone pretending together reinforces their sense of being part of the group.

♦ Because this is such a novel experience for many, it's an opportunity to modify their responses so that their excitement does not make them so wild that they are not able to stand and be part of the sandwich.

♦ There is also the culinary lesson being learned about what goes into a good sandwich (not including, of course, the rice and chocolate combo!).

MODIFICATIONS

♦ For children who need visual input, show appropriate pictures of sandwiches and ingredients, and place footprints or a line of tape on the floor to show them where to stand when they are sandwich ingredients. You can also place pictures of the sandwich ingredients on the floor so the child who is a pickle will know where to stand and what he is supposed to be.

♦ When asking the children, "What else shall we put in this sandwich?" offer several pictures and let them choose the ones they want.

♦ For children who are hypersensitive to touch, have them be the bread so that they are only touched on one side. Or, if even that is too much, have them be the person squeezing the others or have them be the "eaters" of the sandwich.

♦ For those who are just watching, keep their interest and encourage them to stay with the group by giving them pictures of the food to look at, or have an adult hold the watching child in a firm and comforting embrace while commenting on the action he is watching: "Now Jacob is pretending to be a piece of cheese in the sandwich."

♦ For the child who needs more tactile stimulation to stay present, pretend to smear mustard or other condiments on him by rubbing your hand down his back.

Are You My Mummy?

With a simple piece of material, you can turn a child into a fun monster.

GOALS

Playing with others
Proprioceptive stimulation
Vestibular stimulation
Imagination

MATERIALS

Ace bandages, elastic
    therapy bands, or a long scarf

SETUP

Unroll the bandage to get it ready to wrap a child.

DIRECTIONS

Have one child stand still while the other children, with an adult directing, wrap the bandage around the child's body. Mime a mummy's stiff-legged walk for the wrapped child to imitate. Demonstrate funny sounds to accompany the walk.

VARIATIONS

1. Wrap a body part instead and make the activity one of a doctor and patient. The doctor is fixing the patient's arm or leg.

2. Wrap an inanimate object instead, such as a teddy bear, and turn it into a mummy that chases after the other kids.

WHAT IS BEING LEARNED

♦ The pressure of the bandage can be very comforting to children who are seeking proprioceptive input. Having to walk while wrapped challenges their balancing skills.

♦ Wrapping others up can make them aware that other children have similar body parts and that they enjoy the tactile input of touching and being touched.

♦ If the variations are played, children also get a chance to use their imaginations and pretend to be a doctor, patient, or scared kid running from a pretend mummy.

MODIFICATIONS

♦ The temperament of the child determines whether the whole body is wrapped, whether the arms are included in the wrapping, or whether just one body part is wrapped. Some children seek out deep touch, while others avoid it. Let that awareness help you decide what is wrapped, who is the wrapper, and who is the wrapped one.

Balloon Baseball

Balloons are always one of the best toys because they attract attention and are light and easy to play with. This game uses the balloon as the ball in baseball. The balloon moves so slowly that beginners can more easily hit it.

GOALS

Eye-hand coordination
Awareness of roles
Focusing
Motor planning
Modulation
Spatial awareness
Vestibular stimulation

MATERIALS

Newspaper sections
Tape
Balloons

SETUP

Make newspaper bats by rolling up sections of newspaper and taping them. The more newspaper sections, the bigger the bat.

DIRECTIONS

An adult throws a balloon toward the child with the bat. Encourage the child to hit the balloon or have an adult stand behind the child and physically prompt him on timing. When the balloon is hit, encourage the other children to try to catch the balloon. Have children take turns being pitcher, batter, catcher, and fielders.

WHAT IS BEING LEARNED

◆ Children are learning to coordinate their movements and timing to connect with the balloon. They can see the results of their movements and then modify their actions to get the desired consequence.

◆ They are learning that everyone has a different role. Someone throws, another bats, and others catch.

◆ Their balance and spatial awareness are being challenged as they run while looking up to catch the balloon, and to the sides to avoid banging into others.

MODIFICATIONS

◆ Some children will have difficulty tracking the balloon in order to catch it. They might get distracted or lose interest and need verbal cues to stay on task.

◆ Children who have difficulty with timing and eye-hand coordination will need hand-over-hand assistance.

Blanket Ride

Giving and getting rides on a blanket can be a fun way of being with others. In this game, all you need is a sturdy piece of cloth and a smooth floor to create a nice give-and-take experience.

GOALS

Awareness of others
Purposeful activity with another
Balance
Strength
Proprioceptive input
Vestibular stimulation
Awareness of cause and effect

MATERIALS

Small blanket(s) or sturdy piece of material
Smooth floor

SETUP

Clear the floor of objects and set one or more blankets or cloths on the floor.

DIRECTIONS

Put one child on the blanket and have another child and an adult, if help is needed, pull it so that the child gets a ride.

Swoosh the blanket this way and that way in unexpected directions to make the ride more exciting, but make sure the ride doesn't get wild enough to throw the child off. Add fun sounds for the kids to imitate.

Have the children switch positions. The one who was sitting is now the puller and vice versa.

Sometimes, make it a group activity. Have two or more children riding together and two or more pulling!

Sometimes, have the children spin the child by running in a circle, rather than asking them to pull the blanket.

VARIATIONS

1. A cardboard box works well when one child sits inside and the other pushes or pulls it across the floor or spins it in a circle.

2. A wagon also achieves these goals, but needs more careful monitoring by the adult.

3. An office chair on wheels also can be used and is great for spinning.

4. A boogie board can also be used, using the leash to pull it.

5. Use several blankets so that many rides are being taken at once, requiring the pullers to watch out for the others and aim for the empty spaces in the room.

WHAT IS BEING LEARNED

♦ Children are learning that they can be responsible for another person's pleasure. They can also see, when being pulled by another, that others can be a source of fun for them as well.

♦ When children are sitting together and being pulled, they get jostled and lean on each other, becoming more aware of the other children.

♦ While sitting on a moving blanket, children are getting experience with balance. In order to stay seated upright while being jiggled and moved in various directions, they have to continually adjust their trunk muscles.

♦ Children who are pulling strengthen their muscles, especially those in their arms and legs.

♦ Spinning is a great source of vestibular input; and if the spinning is stopped and started at intervals, it stimulates feedback from the child's inner ear.

♦ If you use several blankets so that many rides are being taken at once, help children avoid running into each other by giving the instruction "Go into the empty spaces."

MODIFICATIONS

♦ For children who are generally not aware of other children, emphasize what is happening with words and touch. Pull the blanket with your learner and walk backward or stop after a few steps and say, "Look! We're giving Oliver a ride!" It generally helps to accompany the words with a hug or little squeeze to increase alertness.

♦ Riding together and bumping into others may be difficult for some kids. Start them off with only one other child and go slowly. At the other extreme are the children who crave a lot of physical touch—riding fast with others falling on them and over them is just what they like and need. This is a game that can accommodate everyone.

♦ Monitor for sensory overload, such as increased distractibility or confusion, rapid breathing, or sweaty skin, and stop the activity if these occur. Provide deep-pressure input to normalize the arousal level.

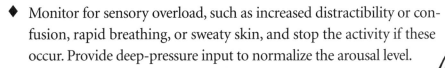

Boat Ride

Unexpected movements can provide many possibilities for fun and motor skill development.

GOALS

Tolerating the unexpected
Pretend play
Increasing language skills

MATERIALS

Large box
Optional: pictures of a boat (or train, bus, or car)

SETUP

Set the opened box on the floor.

DIRECTIONS

Announce to the children that it is time for a boat ride and have one or more of them sit inside the box.

Sing "Row, Row, Row Your Boat."
Say, "Uh-oh. There's a storm. Hold on," as you start rocking the box back and forth.
Say, "Oh—the waves are big!" as you rock a little harder.
Say, "Whew, the storm is over," stop rocking, and sing "Row, Row, Row Your Boat" again.

VARIATIONS

1. Instead of a boat, pretend it's a train or a bus or a car that is pulled or pushed along the floor.

2. Instead of rocking, have the train alternate between very fast and very slow or between stops and starts.

WHAT IS BEING LEARNED

♦ Children are experiencing the unexpected. They are discovering that sometimes they have no control over what happens and it can be OK.

♦ They are learning such concepts as fast and slow, stop and go, and in and out, and if encouraged to say these words to control the activity, they are increasing their communication skills.

♦ They are, of course, learning to play pretend and imagine that inanimate objects are other things.

MODIFICATIONS

♦ Begin the rocking slowly to see how it is tolerated. If the children seem to enjoy it, increase the rocking.

♦ If a large box rocks too much, use a smaller box.

♦ If one child seems uncomfortable, *before* he melts down, act as if the boat has arrived at a port and one passenger needs to disembark. Make his leaving part of the game. Later, make a pretend stop and see if he wants to get back on. Or encourage the child to say, "Stop!" or put his hand out to gesture "stop," giving him some control over the movement.

♦ For children who are new at pretending and building their imaginations, show them a picture of a boat so that they can see that this is not a box, but a pretend boat (or train, bus, or car).

♦ For the child who has gravitational insecurity and needs stability or tactile pressure, have an adult go in the box if possible to hold him.

♦ For the child who is hypersensitive to touch, place him in the boat by himself for few sessions before adding others.

Box Ride

A plain brown box from a local grocery store can provide an activity that works on motor skills and offers an opportunity to move others.

GOALS

Turn taking
Understanding rules
Balance

Cooperation
Awareness of others

MATERIALS

Medium-size cardboard box

SETUP

Set the open box on a cleared floor.

DIRECTIONS

Put one child in the box. Tell one or more children that they, with your help, are going to move the box and give the child a ride by pulling it around the room. You can pretend that it's a car getting towed or a boat on the water.

Depending on the weight of the child, the box can be easy or hard to push, and it might work better to pull it. Try it both ways, emphasizing the need to figure out which way works better. For example, say, "Help me push the box. Let's give Kailani a ride. Oh, it's too hard to push. How are we going to move her?"

WHAT IS BEING LEARNED

♦ The object of the game is to engage the child in problem solving in a social situation. How should they give the child a ride? Maybe they will come up with the solution of going in a circle. Or the learning can come from watching you solve the problem.

MODIFICATIONS

♦ For some children, just sitting in a box or getting in and out of a box is plenty of activity.

♦ Some children might prefer to turn the boxes over and hide under them. You can change the game into hide-and-seek, pretending not to have a clue where they hid and then finding them!

Going Through the Tunnel of Legs

This is a good game to get adults involved in the play. Parents and older siblings are definitely welcomed. All that the big people have to do is stand in a line, feet apart, and form a tunnel. The children crawl through the legs. The big people have the power, if they want, to make the tunnel narrower and narrower. Maybe even take a toll?

GOALS

Understanding beginning and end
Adjusting one's body to spaces of different sizes
Being part of a group
Experiencing getting in line behind others
Awareness of other bodies and allowing them into their space
Increasing proprioceptive input

MATERIALS

Three or more adults

SETUP

The adults stand in a line behind each other with their legs open in a V formation.

DIRECTIONS

The children are encouraged to get on all fours and crawl through the legs of the adults. Keep control of the traffic by having another adult at the end of the tunnel directing children back to the beginning. Otherwise children might try to crawl back the way they came, which makes for an interesting traffic jam but is less comfortable for the bridge parts.

Once the children have the idea of the game, modify it by narrowing the stance of the adults so that the space to crawl through is narrower. In order to get through, children have to modify their positions and tilt their bodies sideways.

Sing a song while children are crawling to whatever tune you want:

> Crawling through the tunnel
> Crawling through the tunnel
> Crawling through the tunnel
> All the way to the end

VARIATIONS

1. Keep bringing the legs closer and closer together so that the crawlers have to turn sideways to squeeze through.

2. Use a line of chairs for the children to crawl under.

3. Use a series of tables to crawl under.

4. Have bigger children make a tunnel for the smaller ones.

WHAT IS BEING LEARNED

♦ Children are learning to adjust their bodies to fit into the space, and if they try to walk upright through the tunnel of legs, they won't fit.

♦ If the variation is played in which the tunnel is made smaller, children become aware of a difference in space and learn that they need to make the physical adjustment in their bodies by turning sideways to fit.

♦ Children are also learning that when something ends, it is possible to go back to the beginning and do it again.

MODIFICATIONS

♦ Some children will try to crawl through the tunnel at the same moment as another. They might need some physical prompting to wait, with encouraging words, such as "Your turn is coming. Almost your turn. Now, it's your turn. Good waiting!"

♦ Some children will need help turning their bodies sideways when the opening is narrowed, or they will keep jamming their shoulders against the legs and not understand why they can't go forward.

♦ It's also important to have an adult at the end directing the children back to the beginning to prevent the children who get easily distracted from leaving the game.

Hammock Swing

There's a reason why infants like to be rocked. It's very soothing. This game can elicit that calming feeling or be a source of alert, wild delight. The kids decide. We comply.

GOALS

Trusting others
Helping others have a pleasant experience
Waiting for one's turn
Gaining strength
Vestibular input

MATERIALS

Blanket or sturdy cloth

SETUP

Lay the blanket on the floor.

DIRECTIONS

Have two adults hold either side of the blanket. Have one child lie on the cloth. The adults pick up the cloth so that the child is suspended, then slowly rock the cloth from side to side.

Other children are encouraged to help hold the cloth and rock the child.

Sing "Rock-a-Bye Baby" as you rock.

On the words "Down will come baby, cradle and all," gently lower the child to the ground.

Give the next child a turn.

VARIATIONS

1. For the child who enjoys unexpected movements, jiggle the hammock in unexpected ways and increase the speed. Try different variations and see which ones bring on calmness and which ones produce giggles.

2. Let two children swing in the hammock together.

3. Instead of swinging or jiggling, bounce the child up and down as if on a trampoline.

4. You and the child can give a teddy bear or other toy a hammock ride.

WHAT IS BEING LEARNED

◆ While being rocked gently, children who tend to be anxious are provided an opportunity to know what being calm feels like.

- Children are also having the experience of trusting others and learning that other people can be a source of pleasure and fun.
- If they help hold the blanket to rock another, they are increasing their awareness of their ability to give pleasure to others. They are also gaining muscle strength from holding the blanket. (So are the adults. Who needs to lift weights at a gym?)
- Children may clamor to have turns, which makes this another good opportunity to experience waiting for one's turn. And while waiting, they can be providing the fun for another by helping to rock the hammock.

MODIFICATIONS

- The children who are helping to rock may need a lot of physical guidance on how to rock the blanket in ways that are soothing to everyone.
- A child who feels insecure lying down may feel more in control if sitting on the hammock while being gently and slowly rocked. Swinging that is slow and rhythmic is usually calming, whereas fast, erratic swinging is alerting to the nervous system. If slow and rhythmic is best, sing lullaby songs to set the pace.
- Monitor the child's reaction. Stop the swing sometimes to allow her to integrate the sensations from her inner ear. A child who is underreactive to her vestibular system may want a lot of fast movements and then may become overloaded. By paying attention to her reaction, you can stop before she reaches that point.

Hit the Homemade Piñata

Hitting a piñata is an activity commonly associated with a fiesta, and players wear a blindfold. This version can be played any time and players can watch what they are doing!

GOALS

Focusing
Accomplishing a goal
Eye-hand coordination
Playing with others
Turn taking

MATERIALS

Newspaper
Plastic bag
Rope
Newspaper bat
Optional: bells

SETUP

Squish up some newspaper and put it in a plastic bag to form a round shape. Hang it up from a piece of rope so that the bag hangs free.

Roll up newspaper and tape it closed to form a bat.

If you use bells, hang them on the rope so that they jingle when the bag is hit.

DIRECTIONS

Have children take turns hitting the piñata with the newspaper bat. Encourage the others to say, "Hurray" or clap when the batters are successful and to use phrases like "Good try!" or "Try again!" if they are not.

VARIATIONS

1. Hang a beach ball instead of a newspaper piñata if you want something more colorful.

2. Hang a smaller item inside a clear plastic bag if you want to increase the challenge.

WHAT IS BEING LEARNED

Children are learning to take turns, to notice what others are doing, and to encourage them. They are getting practice in eye-hand coordination and getting the satisfaction of accomplishing a goal.

MODIFICATIONS

Use a hand-over-hand approach for children who are not able to do this independently by standing behind them and placing your hands over theirs on the bat.

Hang bells or other noisemakers on the rope to increase the feedback for children who need additional feedback.

"I'm Here!"

It is difficult for many children with autism to learn to respond to being called by name, to call others, and to greet others. In this game, this social skill can be practiced in less confusing situations.

GOALS

Name recognition
Social response
Auditory and visual stimulation
Increasing language skills

MATERIALS

Large appliance box or large piece of material, such as a sarong or curtain

SETUP

Set up the large box or hang the curtain to block off one part of the room. An adult should then hide behind the box or curtain before the children are there. When the children come into the room, have them, and at least one other adult, sit facing the curtain or box.

DIRECTIONS

An adult in the group models words by calling out to the person who is behind the box or curtain. The name is called with a melodic inflection: "Marissa, where aaaaare you?" Marissa appears and says, "I'm here!" Everyone claps and smiles and says, "Hi Marissa!"

Do this with several people to provide a model and then have each child take a turn.

VARIATIONS

1. Use stuffed animals hiding behind a box and call out, "Giraffe, where aaaaare you?" and bring it in front of the box and say, "Hi!"

2. Use a book of animal pictures and call out each name, "Polar bear where aaaaare you?" Open the page to the polar bear picture and say hello or kiss the picture. Or, have a child look through the book and find the picture.

WHAT IS BEING LEARNED

♦ Children are learning a social response of greeting by saying, "Hi" when someone appears. They are getting an opportunity to practice anticipation. When they hear the words "Where are you?" they learn to expect that someone will appear. They are also learning what words to say when they are looking for someone.

♦ Having the group give a rousing cheer when she appears also has the benefit of making the child feel noticed, appreciated, and loved.

MODIFICATIONS

♦ For the child whose attention might be distracted, increase his awareness of a person appearing from behind the curtain or box by having that person greet the child with a hug or firm touch. Or have the person dance out, use some unusual movement to attract attention, or wear a funny hat.

♦ Children who are unclear on how the game works will need an adult to go behind the curtain with them when it's their turn to hide. The adult should exaggerate listening to the call, such as by turning his head, putting his hand behind his ear and making a listening face, and so on. The adult could also say such words as "Why, that's your name. They are calling for you. Let's go!" Then prompt the child to appear.

♦ Be aware of the child who reacts badly to sudden noises and, instead of clapping, use the sign language for applause and wiggle all ten fingers.

Jump to Colors

Noticing that things are different colors and learning that colors have different names are high on the list of children's first cognitive and visual awareness. This game reinforces that awareness by adding the fun of movement.

GOALS

Eye-foot coordination
Vestibular stimulation
Color identification
Turn taking
Spatial awareness

MATERIALS

Sheets of colored construction paper in two colors

SETUP

Tape the sheets of colored construction paper on the floor in a vertical line, alternating the colors. For example, a red sheet, then a blue one, then red again, and so on, repeating the pattern. Leave a one-inch space between each paper.

DIRECTIONS

Have children start by taking turns jumping from one color to the next saying the names of the colors they are jumping on. Or have an adult say, "Jump to the red. Now jump to the blue," and so forth. Next, children are encouraged to jump to sheets that are all the same color—for example, jumping only on the red ones.

If doing this in groups, verbally or physically prompt the players to return to the beginning and start again so that they don't turn around and run into another child.

Increase the challenge by changing the colors or adding a third color so that jumping to all the green ones can be tricky.

VARIATIONS

1. Draw shapes and tape them on the floor in different patterns. "Jump to the square. Now jump to the circle. Now jump to the triangle."

2. Draw faces. "Jump to the sad face. Now jump to the mad face. Now jump to the happy face."

3. Have two children jump together.

WHAT IS BEING LEARNED

♦ Besides becoming more aware of differences in color, children are learning to jump forward different distances. Jumping up and down in place is motorically different from jumping forward. Jumping forward requires an awareness of the extra energy it takes to move the body forward, as well as the use of body positioning. Accomplishing this task increases children's ability to utilize both their proprioceptive and vestibular (balance) sense.

♦ By returning to the beginning of the line each time, they are developing their spatial awareness. They are seeing the difference between the beginning and the end. Waiting for one's turn is also an element of this game.

MODIFICATIONS

♦ Be prepared to help a child jump using a variety of methods.

♦ For some children, just jumping forward from color to color is enough for now, because their work is in developing the ability to jump rhythmically.

♦ For the children who cannot yet "catch air" beneath their feet when jumping, stand behind and physically lift them up while you both are jumping forward. For the children who are able to jump up but not yet forward, stand beside them, holding hands and jumping together. Repeating rhythmic clues, such as "One, two, three, jump, one, two, three, jump!" can help some children get cognitively ready to move.

♦ If you have an older or more motorically skilled child in the group, have her partner with another by holding hands. The more advanced child jumps backward while the other jumps forward.

Leap the Shoes

I like this game because shoes are always around. You can make the game easy with just a few shoes or quite challenging with a pile of them, so that the game fits the child's skill level. Remember: always start below a child's level. Make it too easy at first. This promotes confidence and self-esteem and is a good warm-up for the body.

GOALS

Tolerating being the center of attention
Adjusting movements to leap longer distances and higher heights

MATERIALS

Shoes

SETUP

Line the children up, one behind the other. Put one shoe in front of the first child. Keep other shoes nearby in easy reach.

DIRECTIONS

Ask the children to jump over the one shoe. Then, for the next turn, add another shoe and have them leap over two shoes. Then three, and so on, until the line of shoes is too long to leap over.

At this point, change the game by making a pile of shoes in the middle of the floor. Now, instead of leaping forward over a line of shoes, they are jumping up over the height of the pile and, instead of standing in one place and jumping over, they are taking a running start. Mark the spot in which to begin the run with a piece of tape. Provide an example by having an adult take a running start and model jumping over the whole pile.

To add to the excitement while someone is running and jumping, have the others do an accompanying drumroll by slapping hands on the floor, table, or knees; say the name of the person when she takes off; and applaud when she lands.

VARIATIONS

1. Use other materials instead of shoes, such as empty milk or juice cartons.

2. Stack cartons in a tower or wall and have each child run and kick it down rather than jump over it. Children can take turns stacking the cartons back up.

WHAT IS BEING LEARNED

♦ On the motoric level, children are learning how much energy they need to use in order to leap off the ground. They learn to anticipate at which point in their running stride they need to take off in order to make the leap. This awareness teaches them self-regulation as well as praxia, the ability to plan one's movements.

- If they are doing drumrolls, they are getting an experience in making rhythm, and if they jump at a consistent moment, they are learning about timing.

- On the social level, children are learning to take turns. They are also enjoying being, or allowing themselves to be, the center of attention. The experience of everyone watching them and calling their names can make them feel very noticed and special.

MODIFICATIONS

- Some children will need one or two adults or other children to run with them to give them the feeling of how fast to run and when to leap.

- Some children will straddle the pile rather than jump over it or leap beside it. They may be lacking in strength and coordination. Give these kids extra practice on other days with smaller piles.

Massages

Massaging is an effective way to help the mind-brain-body self-organize. Massaging is done in long, firm strokes to the children's arms, legs, and backs to increase their awareness of their bodies, stimulate their tactile systems, and to help them be mindful of the moment.

GOALS

Tactile stimulation
Decreasing tactile defensiveness
Body awareness
Mind-body organization
Calming

MATERIALS

None

SETUP

The adult is sitting on the floor, and the child is sitting comfortably between the adult's legs.

DIRECTIONS

Starting at a shoulder, stroke your hand downward toward the hand while singing (to the tune of "Here We Go 'Round the Mulberry Bush"):

This is the way we rub our arms

Rub our arms, rub our arms

This is the way we rub our arms

Early in the morning

Continue with the other arm, and then the hands, legs, feet, and back. Change the words to the song accordingly.

VARIATIONS

1. Have the child massage the adult, encouraging him to stroke the part of the body named in the song.

2. Have children massage each other with help from the adult, if needed.

3. Use such materials as a loofah or nylon bath scrubby.

WHAT IS BEING LEARNED

♦ Massages used at the beginning of the session can help the mind-brain-body self-organize by stimulating the peripheral nervous system. This helps improve the ability to pay attention.

♦ Massages tend to be calming and organizing to a child's central nervous system. As the child receives deep-touch pressure to the skin, the tactile receptors that are overresponsive to light or touch are depressed. In time, the child who is tactilely defensive may respond more appropriately to overall tactile stimulation, and can then enjoy such activities as playing with Play-Doh, finger painting, and so on, as well as being in closer proximity to other children.

MODIFICATIONS

♦ For children who are uncomfortable with being massaged, try gently squeezing the arms and leg muscles instead.

♦ Monitor the child's reaction so that she is never pushed past her limits of tolerating the activity.

♦ To encourage more communication and allow a child more control, ask which body parts he wants massaged next. Use a picture board, gestures, or pointing if speech is delayed.

Name Game

Being aware of others can start with the awareness that others have names. This game uses a ball to encourage this awareness.

GOALS

Awareness of others
Proprioceptive stimulation
Attentive endurance

MATERIALS

Ball

SETUP

Have the players sit in a circle. If physical prompting is needed, have a child sit between an adult's legs, or beside an adult or other child.

DIRECTIONS

Players roll a ball to each other. Before rolling the ball, each player says the name of or looks at the person the ball is being rolled to.

VARIATIONS

Use the same method of saying each player's name before the following actions:

1. Stand in a circle and bounce the ball to each other.

2. Stand in a circle and pass the ball to the person on the right.

WHAT IS BEING LEARNED

- ◆ Children are learning the names of others in the group. They are learning to stay attentive for longer periods as they watch and wait for their turn.

- ◆ Motorically, they are learning which muscles are needed to roll the ball in the direction desired. They are experiencing rolling (or throwing or bouncing) the ball in the correct direction through the proprioceptive feedback.

MODIFICATIONS

♦ Some children have difficulty staying seated. To help, apply some pressure when they are sitting between your legs so that they are sitting snugly and will be less likely to get distracted and leave the area. The snugness gives their body feedback and helps them attend.

♦ If sitting is still a problem, stand up to play the game and help the child jump up and down while waiting for a turn. Jumping releases excess energy and makes it easier to stay with an activity.

♦ In the beginning, especially, it will be necessary for the adult to say the names and help some children throw in the correct direction.

Obstacle Course

Moving one's body in a variety of ways is what develops flexibility and motor planning. In setting up this obstacle course, think prepositionally and have things to go over, under, around, and through.

GOALS

Motor planning
Flexibility
Understanding prepositions
Balance
Discrimination
Modulation
Changing positions

MATERIALS

There are many obstacle course options. Here are a few of them:

A short balance beam or a 2 × 4 or 2 × 6 board
Object to climb over, such as a chair, stool, or pile of cushions

Object to crawl under, such as a table or rope

Object to crawl through, such as a hula hoop on its side or cloth tunnel

Objects to jump on, such as colored paper and small trampolines

SETUP

Arrange the objects in such a way that children go directly from one obstacle to another and end up back at the beginning so they can do it again. A balance beam is a good piece to begin with. Then have children go from there to, for example, a short stool that they need to step up on and jump down from. Next have a table, which they will need to crawl under. Then set up a hula hoop or box propped on its side, which they will need to bend down to go through, ending up back at the balance beam.

DIRECTIONS

Have children start at the first obstacle and, for each object, tell them or model how to go over, under, through, and so forth.

VARIATIONS

1. Use different movements, such as walking sideways or backward.

2. Change the obstacles once a month to present new challenges or rearrange the obstacles in a different configuration.

3. Increase the social aspect by having children hold hands and go together. Or have the children stand in a line behind each other with hands on the shoulders or around the waist of the person in front.

4. Let the children rearrange the objects to make up their own course.

5. Add a fine motor activity, such as stacking blocks using tongs, in the middle of the course so that children interrupt their gross motor activity to do something that requires finesse. A cognitive activity, such as matching colors, could be used instead.

WHAT IS BEING LEARNED

♦ There is so much learning taking place in an obstacle course. Every time the children have to adjust their posture to make a new move, they are increasing their balance, flexibility, and ability to distinguish between similar movements and modulate accordingly. For example, jumping forward and jumping on a trampoline are both jumping skills that use slightly different movements.

♦ Their understanding of language increases by physically experiencing, for example, the difference between under and over. Verbal requests, such as "Please get the ball that's under the shelf," will thus have more meaning.

♦ If you send children through the obstacle course fairly quickly one after the other, every time someone moves too quickly or too slowly, they learn about spatial relationships where only one person can be in a space at a time!

MODIFICATIONS

♦ Children can be given as much or as little assistance as needed. Some children will need such help as supporting arms around their waist or physical and verbal prompts to bend down, stand up, or climb on.

♦ Other children will need to be more challenged so they won't be bored. Have them walk and jump and bend backward or do the whole course with their hands in their pockets.

♦ Children who need heavy work to feel calmer should be encouraged to move the obstacles to make up their own course or help you set up the course.

Races

This is an everyone-wins race.

GOALS

Following directions
Anticipating a goal
Motor planning (conscious use of muscles to achieve a goal)
Awareness of others

MATERIALS

None

SETUP

If this game is played with two adults, the adults face each other with the child standing in front of one adult and facing the other.

If played in a small group, the adults form parallel lines. The children stand in front of one line of adults, facing the other line.

DIRECTIONS

Give the instruction "Run to . . . " using whatever name identifies the other adult.

Give as much or as little help as needed to propel the child in the right direction, while the other adult also does encouraging sounds and movements, for example, holding her arms open at child's level, calling the child's name, and so on.

When the child reaches the goal of arriving at the other person, make a big deal. "You did it!" "Good running!" "Yea!"

Have the child run back and forth between the adults for a while.

VARIATIONS

1. In subsequent sessions, enlarge the distance between the adults.

2. Change the movement, such as jumping between adults or running backward.

WHAT IS BEING LEARNED

♦ The child is having the experience of following directions, achieving a goal, and having that success recognized by the hoots and hollers of the adults. There is increased social awareness in both pleasing others and the pleasure of receiving praise.

MODIFICATIONS

♦ Children who are hypersensitive to sounds may need to have the hooting and hollering toned down or to receive other forms of praise, such as a firm hug.

Rolling Children

You'd think having a body roll over yours would feel uncomfortably heavy. But, for many children, the temporary weight can instead be a form of comfort.

GOALS

Awareness of others
Proprioceptive feedback
Experiencing novelty

MATERIALS

Carpeted floor

SETUP

Have children lie on their backs, lined up next to each other with the sides of their bodies touching.

DIRECTIONS

Roll the child from one end, on top of all the other children, to the other end of the line. Then roll the next child over all the others. Continue until the first child is at the beginning of the line again. Then reverse direction and repeat the game, returning to the original positions.

Sing or chant simple words while the child is rolling, such as:

Rolling, rolling, rolling,
All the way to the end.

VARIATIONS

1. Play this game with a theme, such as Rolling Logs to Market. Or, if played on a special occasion, such as Halloween, Pumpkin Rolling in the Field.

2. Have the child lie on top of the others and perpendicular to them. Then have the children on the bottom all roll in the same direction. This will cause the child on top to move.

WHAT IS BEING LEARNED

♦ Briefly feeling the weight of the passing body gives children proprioceptive feedback that increases their awareness of others and can produce a calm alertness or a giggle fit.

♦ Experiencing the novelty of the new situation also captures children's attention and lets them see that they can do something completely new that could be a positive experience.

♦ The game also could help them feel that they are part of a group as they each have a turn experiencing all the others rolling over them.

MODIFICATIONS

♦ The child who is hypersensitive to touch, possibly making him very uncomfortable in this situation, can be encouraged to sit and

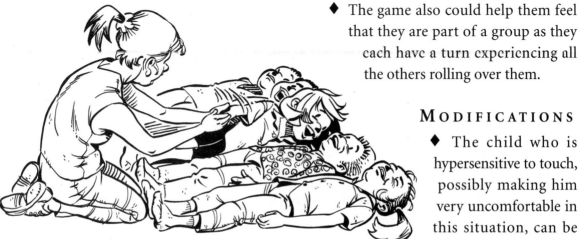

watch and sing. An adult can be with this child, describing the action: "Jay is going to roll next." Or use this as an opportunity for the child to identify his classmate: "Who's rolling now? You're right, it's Jay!"

RurRurRurRurRUN!

The anticipation of taking off at a fast run can be as enjoyable as the run itself.

GOALS

Imitation
Listening for cues
Vestibular, auditory, and proprioceptive stimulation

MATERIALS

None

SETUP

Stand children in a line between the adults and have everybody hold hands.

DIRECTIONS

Have adults paw the ground with one foot while repeating the phonetic sound of "R" ("RurRurRurRur"). Exaggerate the sound and the movement to capture the children's attention. Ask children to imagine they are horses pawing the ground in anticipation of a run. After four or five paws, say, or shout, "RUN!"

Have everyone together run a short distance and then say, "STOP!" Repeat the game several times, pawing the ground between runs.

VARIATIONS

1. Vary the amount of pawing so the children have to listen for the word "Run!"

2. Vary the number of repetitions and the distance to run.

3. Instead of a group line, play the game with separate pairs or threesomes so that children with similar energy levels can play together.

WHAT IS BEING LEARNED

♦ Children are learning to watch what others are doing and imitate that movement.

♦ They are learning to anticipate what is going to happen next.

♦ They are also learning how to watch for cues to give them information.

♦ The sudden stops and anticipatory starts alert the children's sensory systems and promote attention.

♦ The predictability of the game (movement follows the pawing) also promotes a sense of familiarity that is reassuring.

MODIFICATIONS

♦ For very active children who seek increased sensory input, individually running further and faster with them is a good way to use up a lot of their excess energy.

♦ Children who have a lower response to movement or are unsure how to move on cue can run between two adults or other children, or they can jump instead of running to give them more proprioceptive feedback.

Sausage Roll (or Sushi Wrap, Hot Dog, Burrito . . .)

Young babies are swaddled because it can remind them of the time when they were snug in the womb. This game can bring similar pleasure. Use whatever name is most familiar to each child's culture.

GOALS

Vestibular, proprioceptive, and tactile stimulation
Body awareness
Joint attention
Playing pretend

MATERIALS

Sturdy piece of cloth

SETUP

Lay the cloth down on a rug.

DIRECTIONS

Have one child lie on one end of the cloth. Get the other children to help roll the child from one end of the cloth to the other so he ends up rolled nice and snug inside the cloth.

Sing a song while rolling, such as this one, to the tune of "Row, Row, Row Your Boat":

Roll, roll, roll you up
Roll and roll you up
Roll and roll and roll and roll
Into a delicious sausage [or sushi or tamale . . .]

Then, if you think the child will be amused (as opposed to scared!), have others pretend to eat them up, with adults modeling movements.

"Yum yum!"

Next ask the child, "Ready to be unrolled?"

When ready, gently lift one end of the cloth so the child slowly rolls out onto the rug.

VARIATIONS

1. Do the game standing up.

2. Wrap up two children together.

3. Have several children stand and do a group hug. Then wrap them all up in a large piece of cloth that will go around them more than once.

4. If you pretend they are hot dogs, pretend to rub them with a variety of condiments, such as mustard and relish, using different ways of rubbing for each kind. A sushi roll might have soy sauce and wasabi; burritos, hot sauce and grated cheese.

WHAT IS BEING LEARNED

♦ Children with ASD often really enjoy being snug and cozy in enclosed places. You are recreating that sense of containment and familiar comfort that babies have in the womb. This experience can reinforce that feeling, so that when the child is upset, he can learn to seek out a cozy spot to self-calm.

♦ This is a game that can be used individually, as needed, for a child who is feeling disorganized and is being a loose cannon in the room. This game will give her a moment to get reorganized.

♦ The children who are rolling the "food" can see how they can help another have fun.

♦ If they pretend to be eating the sausage or other "food," children can get more experience in playing pretend and using their imaginations.

MODIFICATIONS

♦ For a child with vestibular issues who may not be sufficiently aware of her head position to adjust it accordingly, take care that her head doesn't get banged when unrolling.

♦ Some children would prefer to have their whole bodies wrapped, including their heads, to enjoy the feeling of dark enclosures.

♦ If a child is at first hesitant with this game, try rolling him in a cloth while standing so he can see if he wants the feeling of snugness.

Scarf Toss

Catching a ball can be difficult for a child just learning eye-hand coordination. Catching a falling scarf, which moves so much more slowly than a ball, is a better way to practice catching.

GOALS

Eye-hand coordination
Playing with a partner
Back-and-forth exchange
Vocabulary
Visual and proprioceptive stimulation

MATERIALS

Scarf

SETUP

Sit directly in front of a child and toss the scarf up. Catch it and say, "I caught it." Do this several times.

DIRECTIONS

Toss the scarf up in the air again and ask the child to catch it. When she catches it, say, "You caught it!"

Start by keeping the tosses low so that the scarf always stays in view as it floats down. Later, toss higher so that the child has to follow the scarf by looking up.

Work toward tossing the scarf back and forth between you. Let her also experiment with tossing the scarf to herself.

VARIATIONS

1. Rather than catching the scarf, let it float gently down into waiting hands.

2. Play the game standing and encourage jumping up to get the scarf while it is still overhead.

WHAT IS BEING LEARNED

♦ Children are learning about timing as well as eye-hand coordination. They have to attend to the trajectory of the falling scarf and figure out when it's the right moment to catch in order to be successful. Later, they will transfer that awareness and timing to catching a ball.

♦ They are experiencing a back-and-forth exchange with another as a form of taking turns. First they have a turn to catch and then a turn to toss.

MODIFICATIONS

♦ For the child who gets distracted, use verbal cues to keep the child focused on the scarf. Remember to start low so that, at first, the scarf is always close to the child's eye level. If needed, have another adult sitting behind the child to do a hand-over-hand approach to help catch the scarf.

♦ For the child who takes longer to process instructions, keep the verbal instructions simple, such as "Catch scarf" and "Toss scarf."

Shape Targets

Examples of shapes are everywhere. In this game, children see the shapes in everyday things and get a chance to identify them by doing a favorite kid action, throwing.

GOALS

Identifying shapes
Increased awareness of environment

MATERIALS

Cut-out side of a large cardboard box
Colored markers
Ball (size depending on skill level of child)

DIRECTIONS

Draw lines on the cardboard box side to divide it into four sections. In each section draw a shape. Use shapes that include those your child already knows and one or two new ones. Add details that make the shape into common sights such as:

A circle could be a sun
A triangle, the sail of a boat
A rectangle, a window
A square, a present with a bow
An oval, a face
An octagon, a stop sign
A trapezoid, the roof of a house
A star, a starfish

Give a child the ball and ask her to try to hit a particular shape.

VARIATIONS

1. Use chalk and draw the shapes on a sidewalk or concrete wall.

2. Have children draw pictures of shapes on paper and tape the papers on the wall.

WHAT IS BEING LEARNED

♦ Children are learning to notice details and see how the information they are learning relates to their lives. This can lead to excitement about looking for other shapes in their lives.

♦ The distance from the shapes and the size of the ball affect the extent of the challenge to eye-hand coordination. Always start at or below their skill level and make it increasingly harder.

MODIFICATIONS

♦ When first presenting the game to someone who doesn't know the shapes yet, name the object she is to throw at instead, for example, "Throw your ball at the sun."

Stack the Cans

There are many ways to use the simple and ubiquitous soda can. A pile of cans is easy to collect, and they can provide many moments of group fun as well as a physical challenge.

GOALS

Working cooperatively
Awareness of cause and effect
Eye-hand coordination
Modulation
Awareness of others
Visual discrimination

MATERIALS

Ten clean, empty aluminum cans
Ball
Basket, such as a laundry basket, or a box

SETUP

Put the cans in the basket or box. Make sure there are no sharp edges on the cans.

DIRECTIONS

Give each child a can. Have children stack cans on top of each other to form a tower. Encourage children to take turns putting a can on the stack and getting another can from the basket. Once the cans are stacked, choose a child to knock them down by rolling the ball. If he knocks them down, applaud and praise him. If he misses, say, "Almost did it! Try again."

After everyone stacks them back up, another child gets a turn to roll the ball.

VARIATIONS

1. Use balls of differing sizes to increase the challenge. A large therapy or exercise ball will require less skill than a beach ball. A tennis ball is more challenging.

2. Put the cans in different positions. For example, place the cans individually on the floor, spaced a little bit apart so that each can needs to be knocked down separately. Or stack the cans like a wall, three tiers high, to make it easy to hit.

3. Use empty plastic water bottles instead of aluminum cans and place the bottles in a line or pyramid formation (as in a real bowling game).

4. Have children kick the cans down instead of using a ball.

WHAT IS BEING LEARNED

♦ Children are learning to do an activity with others to accomplish a goal. First they stack the cans and then they each get a turn to knock them down. They are noticing the success of another and learning the socially appropriate responses of applauding or vocally praising.

♦ They are learning to stack the cans in a stable tower, which requires that they pay attention to the visual information of seeing whether the cans are aligned.

♦ They are learning to control the direction of a rolled ball.

MODIFICATIONS

♦ For children who need more visual information to understand the goal, show them a picture of what the cans will look like when they are stacked (or placed in a pyramid formation) and then a picture of the cans being knocked down by a ball.

♦ If children have a hard time waiting for their turn to knock the cans down, use a smaller number of cans so they can finish the stacking more quickly. Or do several towers so everyone can knock the cans down at once.

♦ Some children who prefer solitary activities will want to make their own can towers. Try to interrupt and add one or two cans to their towers to help them tolerate allowing others to be part of their activities.

♦ If one or more of the children are more advanced in their social skills, assign them the job of passing out the cans to the other children.

Stop and Go

This game helps teach the ability to stop and start movement quickly, which is crucial to a child's ability to respond to a warning to "Stop!"

GOALS

Motor control

Listening to instruction

Imitation of others

Moving in unison with others

Vestibular, auditory, visual, and proprioceptive stimulation

MATERIALS

Optional: stop sign, green and red colored cloths, bell

SETUP

Children and adults are holding hands while standing in a line. One adult, the leader, is facing the line.

DIRECTIONS

The leader says, "Go" and begins to walk backward while everyone in the line moves forward at a normal pace. She then says, "Stop" and everyone stops immediately. The leader continues these calls while varying the amount of time spent walking or stopping.

This game is especially fun if the adults exaggerate their stopping and starting by coming to an abrupt halt or a speedy start. Because you are holding hands, children can feel the suddenness of the movements.

VARIATIONS

1. The speed of the movement can also be varied depending on how quickly the leader can run backward!

2. Very slow motion is also fun.

3. Try this game in sand at the beach for a different level of challenge.

WHAT IS BEING LEARNED

◆ This game encourages children to listen to directions, watch what others are doing, and imitate them.

♦ They are learning to control their bodies better by being able to start and stop on cue.

♦ They are also experiencing being part of a group and being in sync with others.

♦ If you do this game at the beach, the unevenness of the sandy terrain challenges their ability to balance and stimulates their vestibular systems.

MODIFICATIONS

♦ Some children may need additional verbal or auditory cues, such as having the other adults repeating the words "Go" or "Let's go!" and "Stop" or "Time to stop!" after the leader says them.

♦ Children who respond more to visual cues may do better if a red scarf is waved or a stop sign held up when it is time to stop, and a green scarf or sign is used when it is time to go.

♦ Children who are more independent can be allowed to play without having their hands held.

Target Games

The eye-hand coordination required for throwing is one of the most basic motor skills. For children with ASD, who especially need to learn how to transfer their knowledge from one activity to many, throwing games can be done in a variety of ways. This game provides that variety. And doing this skill with others can increase the fun factor, because there is excitement in the air when the ball successfully hits the target. Even adults know the thrill of getting a scrunched-up paper into a wastebasket.

GOALS

Increasing eye-hand coordination
Improving muscle control
Achieving goals

Awareness of others

Visual, proprioceptive, and vestibular stimulation

MATERIALS

Containers, such as open cardboard boxes, plastic bins, or buckets

Objects to throw, such as balls, beanbags, and so forth

SETUP

Set a few containers on the floor and have handy the objects to throw.

DIRECTIONS

Have each child stand in front of a target, or have all the children sit in a circle with the target in the middle. Give each child in turn an object to throw, and have her throw it into or at the target of her choice.

Make each game easier or harder by adjusting the distance between the thrower and the targets.

VARIATIONS

1. Use socks as balls and buckets or dishwashing tubs as the containers.

2. Have children throw checkers into basins. This requires throwing a smaller object, but using a dishwashing basin or tub that has a wide opening makes it easier.

3. Use beanbags and boxes of different sizes.

4. Use Ping-Pong balls and large cans.

5. Use balls and paper targets on the wall.

WHAT IS BEING LEARNED

◆ Children are learning that it is necessary to look at an object in order to be able to throw at it. They are learning the importance of letting their eyes guide their hands in this eye-hand coordination game.

◆ They are also learning how to control and grade their muscle strength to achieve specific physical goals of throwing farther, higher, or harder.

MODIFICATIONS

♦ Some children will only throw by walking up to the target and dropping it. They have not yet learned how to use their arm to project. Help them learn by holding them a short distance from the object and, using hand-over-hand, guide their hands through the throwing motion. Give verbal cues for letting go of the ball at the right moment by saying, "Open your hand." This is a more concrete clue than "Let go."

♦ Some children look in directions other than where they are throwing. Give them the verbal cue, "Look at the box [or name of target]."

Throw the Balls into the Box

This game has the element of surprise. At first the kids are surprised when a barrage of balls appears out of the bottom of the box. Even after this effect is long gone, the anticipation of the next round makes the experience even more fun.

GOALS

Anticipating results
Understanding prepositional concepts of inside, behind, beside, and so on
Increasing eye-hand coordination
Tolerating the unexpected

MATERIALS

At least two balls per player (children can make their own homemade balls out of newspaper)
Medium-size cardboard box

SETUP

Give each child a section of newspaper to scrunch up into a ball. Put tape around the ball to keep its round shape. Remove the tape from the bottom flaps of the box and then loosely close them.

Open the top flaps of the box. Place the open box on the floor.

DIRECTIONS

Sing the song below, or your own version, and while singing, have the children throw the balls into the box. Allow them to stand as close or as far away from the box as needed to be successful.

(Sung to the tune of "Mary Had a Little Lamb")

> Throw the balls into the box
>
> Into the box
>
> Into the box
>
> Throw the balls into the box
>
> Where did the balls go?

After all the balls are in the box, ask the children,

> "Where are the balls?"
>
> "Are they in front of the box?" (Exaggeratedly look in front of the box.)
>
> Other adults, if needed, cue the kids to say, "No . . ."
>
> "Are they beside the box?" (Again do the same miming on either side of the box.) "No . . ."
>
> "Are they behind the box?" "No . . ."
>
> "Are they inside the box?" (On these last words, lift the box and shake it so all the balls fall out of the bottom of the box. If they don't fall out right away, you may have to give the flaps a little pull, and fold them more loosely next time.)
>
> "Yes!"

The children then run around and collect all the balls. Set the box down again, its bottom flaps loosely folded, and begin the game again. Continue for a few rounds.

VARIATIONS

1. Play this game in the pool using stacked-up inner tubes instead of the box (see next game, Throwing into the Tubes).

2. Use smaller and smaller boxes to challenge the children's eye-hand coordination.

3. Place the box at different distances away from a throwing line (a piece of masking tape or string on the floor could mark a throwing line). The farther away, the greater the skill needed.

4. Use other things to throw: beanbags, Ping-Pong balls, shoes, rolled-up socks, and so on.

WHAT IS BEING LEARNED

♦ On the most basic level, children are practicing their eye-hand coordination and learning the concepts of in front, behind, inside, and beside.

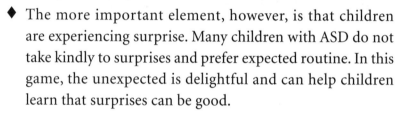

♦ The more important element, however, is that children are experiencing surprise. Many children with ASD do not take kindly to surprises and prefer expected routine. In this game, the unexpected is delightful and can help children learn that surprises can be good.

♦ After playing the game the first time, the anticipation of the surprise enters into the mix, which adds to the pleasure. Of course, some children, like one I worked with once, will not get the point of repeating the game and have to explain to you matter-of-factly that of course the balls are in the box! For children like this it's best to move on to another game before they lose all respect for your intelligence.

MODIFICATIONS

♦ This game can get pretty rowdy and exciting, and could be difficult for children who have severe auditory sensitivities. You might consider using an audible whisper for the singing and the response to make it a quieter but still very effective game.

♦ The game can also be made quieter if children are asked to stand in specific places, and then each child takes a turn to throw.

Throwing into the Tubes

If you played Throw the Balls into the Box, here's a way to transfer that skill to a different setting.

GOALS

Playing with others
Eye-hand coordination
Reinforcing object permanence
Call and response

MATERIALS

Three child-sized inner tubes
Small balls, such as rubber or plastic balls—at least two per child

SETUP

Pile the inner tubes on top of one another in the center of the circle to form a column of tubes with a hole down the center of the column.

DIRECTIONS

Give each child two balls and sing or chant this song (to the tune of "London Bridge Is Falling Down"):

Throw the balls into the tube
Into the tube
Into the tube

Throw the balls into the tube

Where did the balls go?

Then lift up the first inner tube and say, "Are they here?"

Model for the kids to respond, "No!"

Then lift the next tube, and ask again, "Are they here?"

"No!"

Then lift the last tube, which will reveal all the balls. Ask, "Are they here?"

"Yes!"

The children then grab for the balls, and the tubes are replaced so the game can be played again.

VARIATIONS

1. Throw the balls into a plastic sack. Put a hole in the bottom of the sack and lift the sack to let the balls tumble out.

2. Throw the balls into a bucket. Lift up the full bucket and pretend to look under it ("Are they here?"). Then turn the bucket upside down and dump the balls ("Are they here?" "Yes!").

3. Pile the tubes on the water in a pool so that when the last tub is picked up, the balls float free.

WHAT IS BEING LEARNED

♦ Children are participating in a group activity with the goal of throwing all the balls into the column of tubes. They are learning that there is a sequence to the game that includes a call and response. An adult asks, "Are the balls here?" and the response is "Yes" or "No." They are learning to anticipate the lifting of the last tube and getting the excitement of the last tube's being lifted and all the balls' being revealed.

MODIFICATIONS

♦ Children who don't have the coordination or who are easily distracted will need a hand-over-hand approach to throwing the balls into the tubes.

◆ For the child who might throw the balls in other directions than toward the tubes, such as at other children, make sure you are using lightweight balls that will not hurt. Tennis balls should not be used.

◆ A child who is overstimulated by all the excitement can be firmly and lovingly held on an adult's lap to help him stay calm and to provide a safe harbor from which he can participate or watch the action.

Throwing Through the Tube

When you narrow the focus of where to throw, it can be easier to hit the mark. If you have a pool, this game is also lots of fun in the water.

GOALS

Awareness of others
Anticipating action
Eye-hand coordination
Focusing
Visual and proprioceptive stimulation

MATERIALS

Beach ball
Inner tube

SETUP

Two adults hold up the inner tube. Have the children stand on either side of the inner tube, facing the hole.

DIRECTIONS

Give one of the children the beach ball and encourage the children to throw the ball back and forth to each other through the tube. Children new at throwing will often throw the ball every which way. The hole in the tube gives each thrower a clear direction. And when a player throws into the hole, the player on the other side of the tube is in a good position to receive it.

Adults should give as much or as little help as is needed for both catching and throwing.

Because the beach ball is light, there is less fear of being hit.

VARIATIONS

1. Use a hula hoop instead of an inner tube for a larger target.

2. Use a smaller ball to increase the challenge.

3. Do this activity in a pool.

WHAT IS BEING LEARNED

♦ Children are getting the experience of having back-and-forth play with another. The rules of the game are clear and defined by the inner tube. The enthusiasm of the adults can also add to children's feelings of accomplishment as they successfully catch the thrown ball or accurately throw the ball.

♦ Throwing and catching a ball, even a light one, is "heavy" work that increases the child's alertness and body awareness.

♦ If the other children respond happily, the game gives experience in the joy of making others happy.

MODIFICATIONS

♦ If you do this in the pool, the adults may need to physically hold some children up and out of the water so that their arms are in a better position to throw.

♦ Children who need more stimulation to stay alert while waiting for the ball to be returned can subtly have their shoulders and arms squeezed and shoulder joints compressed.

Tug-of-War

This age-old game is a fun way to get to use all your strength and be part of a team. For the child who already has difficulty "pulling his punch," this is a chance to shine by pulling with all his might!

GOALS

Vestibular and proprioceptive stimulation
Awareness of others
Developing strength

MATERIALS

Rope or long, sturdy scarf

SETUP

Children are divided into two groups, one group on each end of the rope. Each player puts both hands on the rope.

DIRECTIONS

When children are in position, call out the verbal cues, "Pull" or "Pull on your rope." Adults on both sides can model the movement and encourage their respective groups to pull hard.

There can be a line on the floor, and the group that crosses it loses. But it's just as fun to pull for the sake of using lots of muscles and to stop when tired!

VARIATIONS

There is only one way to play Tug-of-War, but there could be a variety of things to tug, such as an inner tube or four or five hula hoops tied together so that they don't bend; kids and adults gather around for a group pull.

WHAT IS BEING LEARNED

♦ Children are experiencing what it feels like to use a lot of their strength. This intense use of their muscles increases awareness of their bodies and alerts them to the moment.

♦ They are also getting an opportunity to challenge their sense of balance and learn how to adjust their stance to give themselves support.

♦ Socially, they get the experience of being part of a group and working together.

MODIFICATIONS

♦ This is a particularly good activity for children who are very active, because it gives them a valid place to put their excess energy. If it is difficult for them to not be too rowdy, set up a two-person Tug-of-War and pair two high-energy people together.

Walk with Rhythm

Rhythm is the basis for all smooth movements. Walking to a particular rhythm is a good way to practice rhythmic movement and to become more aware of one's body.

GOALS

Motor control
Differentiating between fast, slow, and stop
Listening to verbal cues
Imitating body movements
Using excess energy
Proprioceptive and vestibular stimulation
Balance
Feeling part of a group

MATERIALS

None

SETUP

Everyone forms a line, holding hands with adults at both ends of the line and in the middle. The adult in the middle is the leader.

DIRECTIONS

The leader says, "Walking, walking, walking" while walking slowly forward. When everyone is walking, the leader stops and says, "Jump," demonstrating and, as needed, helping others to jump.

Next, establish a rhythm to this game. If your group is very active and good at jumping, do a faster four-beat rhythm, such as:

Walking

Walking

Walking

Jump!

A group that needs to do transitions more slowly might do better with an eight-beat rhythm, such as:

Walking

Walking

Walking

Walking

Walking

Walking

Walking

Jump!

VARIATIONS

1. The speed can be anywhere from slow motion to very fast.

2. Movement can also be backward or sideways.

3. Sounds could be used instead of words in order to work on different phonics or to include a child who is at a nonverbal level. For example, "La la la la boing!" (repeat, repeat).

4. Use other commands, such as "Running, running, running, stop" or "Turning, turning, turning, drop!" (Never underestimate a child's delight in falling to the ground. Adults don't always share it!)

5. Try this game in the sand at the beach.

WHAT IS BEING LEARNED

♦ On a motoric level, children are learning which muscles are needed to purposely stop one movement and do a new one. This kind of muscle control helps them to move more smoothly.

♦ On an emotional level, being part of a group, even if it's not yet a cognitive perception, is still felt in the body and can give children a sense of positive connection with others. Chanting sounds or the words together also add to that feeling of camaraderie.

♦ Children who are more aware can be given the role of changing the rhythm or using words of their own to give them a sense of leadership.

♦ When this game is played on the sand or on uneven terrain, the children also get an opportunity to challenge their senses of balance.

MODIFICATIONS

♦ This game is especially good for children who tend to be clumsy and need more work on body awareness. If the variations are also played, it will deepen their awareness.

♦ Children who tend to be anxious about new experiences will begin to calm when the rhythm gets predictable and they can relax in the familiarity. Such variations as walking backward can be done later with the same rhythm so that they can transfer and expand their skills within their new comfort zones.

We Are Rocking

Children who enjoy repetitive motion will especially like this game because it takes them beyond where they could go on their own.

GOALS

Stimulating the vestibular system
Understanding the concepts of fast and slow
Understanding the physical sensation of "stop"

MATERIALS

None

SETUP

Have children stand up with an adult behind each of them.

DIRECTIONS

Holding the child firmly by the hips or trunk, chant the words below while first rocking the child from side to side and, in the second round, forward and backward.

Rock the child just enough to give him the sensation of being off center during the side-to-side and back-and-forth movements and then directly on center on the word "Stop."

(Sung to the tune of "Frère Jacques")

We are rocking, rocking, rocking
We are rocking
Now we stop!

VARIATIONS

1. Do another round of the side-to-side and back-and-forth movements but do it faster. Precede this change with the words "Ready to go faster?"

2. Do another round but this time go very slowly as if in slow motion. Precede this change with the appropriate announcement, "Let's go slower."

3. Play the same game with the child sitting or kneeling.

WHAT IS BEING LEARNED

♦ Children are learning where their centers are by experiencing how it feels to be off center. This information is stored in the inner ear and they begin to process the input, learning to make adjustments to their movements when they feel they are off center and about to fall. This awareness, coming from two kinds of movement, is doubly helpful.

♦ For children who are hyposensitive to this information, having it presented so dramatically increases their awareness.

♦ Children are also experiencing the meaning of "Stop" and what that feels like, so that when they are told to stop (!) at other times in their lives, they will have an internal sense of what that feels like and what is expected.

♦ The game has the concepts of both unpredictability and predictability. As the children get familiar with the game, they know a stop is coming. The unpredictability is in not knowing how fast or how slow the movements will be.

MODIFICATIONS

♦ The forcefulness or the gentleness of the movements can be adjusted to fit individual children. Children who crave more proprioceptive input will like it to be more forceful and will find this movement especially calming and satisfying.

♦ Children who are more defensive will prefer a gentler rocking or would prefer to rock themselves.

♦ Children who want to be independent but find balance a challenge might be more comfortable playing this game while sitting or kneeling rather than standing.

Who Is This?

Recognizing and enjoying one's own reflection and being noticed by others are the essence of this game.

GOALS

Recognizing one self in the mirror
Experiencing the surprise of seeing one's reflection

MATERIALS

Mirror
Scarf

SETUP

Have children sit in a circle and place a mirror in front of one child. Cover the mirror with the scarf.

DIRECTIONS

After the cloth is placed over the mirror, the group chants:

Who is this?
Can anybody tell?
This is (pull the cloth off the mirror and say the child's name) _____
And we like her (him) very well!

VARIATIONS

1. Place a scarf over a child's head instead, and after the song is sung, the scarf is removed to reveal the child.

2. Use stuffed animals instead of children and cover one up at a time.

WHAT IS BEING LEARNED

♦ Children are beginning to notice more facial details so that they can identify and distinguish differences between the people in their lives. Noticing their own facial details is part of this process.

MODIFICATIONS

♦ For children who have difficulty focusing, bring the covered mirror closer or use a larger mirror to capture their attention.

♦ Children who are uncomfortable making eye contact with others might find it easier to look in the mirror. Looking in their own eyes is a good way to practice making eye contact.

Who's in the Box?

If you want a group game that is sure to interest young bodies, bring around a large box and let the fun begin. In this game, children can get the comfort of an enclosed space and often don't mind sharing it.

GOALS

Awareness of others
Learning that others have different names
Enhancing sense of self
Reinforcing object permanence
Learning to enjoy a novel experience

MATERIALS

Large, empty box, such as the kind that appliances come in

SETUP

Place the large box in full view of the children and encourage them to gather around the box and check it out.

DIRECTIONS

After the children have checked the box out, put one child inside the box and have him squat down so you can close the top flaps of the box.

Have the other children gather around the box and chant along with the adults:

> Who's in the box?
> Who's in the box?
> Knock, knock, knock
> Who's in the box?

Children knock on the box on the words "Knock, knock, knock." When the final "Who's in the box?" is said, the top flaps are opened and the child pops up and everyone says that person's name:

> "It's Justin!"

VARIATIONS

1. Put more than one child in the box at one time.

2. Instead of putting the child in the box from the top, cut a door in the side and play the same game.

3. Jiggle the box while the child is inside for extra stimulation.

4. Put large holes in the box so kids can stick an arm out or peer through at the audience.

WHAT IS BEING LEARNED

♦ The game is designed to make children aware that there are other children in the group and that each child has a name.

♦ The game also promotes listening and responding to verbal cues (popping up after hearing, "Who's in the box?" and knocking on the box after hearing the words "Knock, knock, knock").

♦ This box game also allows children to experiment with getting in a new enclosed space and tolerating the newness of the experience.

♦ The children are also reminded that when people aren't seen, they still exist. This awareness can help them become more tolerant of being separated from parents during the day.

♦ Because the game requires turn taking, the children have to learn to wait for their turn and to understand the concept that their turn is coming again.

♦ Because everyone is encouraged to say the name of the child, this game can contribute to the child's sense that he is happily noticed!

MODIFICATIONS

♦ If a child has a hard time waiting for his turn, consider putting two or more children in at the same time. We've put as many as four in a box with great success.

♦ If a child is afraid of the box, place the box on its side and let the child explore it before the game starts.

♦ If a child is anxious about being in the box, modify the game. Start with closing the flaps for only a second and when opening them say, "Peek-a-boo." This makes the game feel more familiar if they have played peek-a-boo games in the past.

♦ Once the comfort level is increased, introduce the longer version.

Wiggling Snake

This can be a very spontaneous game. Although usually played with a rope, it can be played with a string, a cord, or even a long scarf or ribbon. It also can be made to be very easy or very challenging depending upon how quickly you can move!

GOALS

Shared attention
Eye-foot coordination
Timing
Visual, proprioceptive, and vestibular stimulation
Spatial awareness

MATERIALS

Small piece (around two or three feet) of rope, string, cord, scarf, or
ribbon

SETUP

Lay one end of the rope flat on the floor. Hold the other end in your hand.

DIRECTIONS

Challenge your player(s) to step on the end of the rope. When they try,
wiggle it quickly out of the way. Keep challenging them until they step on
the rope.

Move the rope as swiftly or as slowly as needed to keep the players interested, but also successful. Remember to keep one end of the rope always
touching the ground to avoid a swinging, uncontrolled movement.

VARIATIONS

1. Have the children take turns being the one who holds the rope.

2. When the rope is stepped on, encourage the child to keep it down with
   his foot while you try to pull it away. This adds the challenge of main-
   taining balance.

WHAT IS BEING LEARNED

◆ The game encourages children to stay visually focused on the string and
  on their attempts to step on it and stop its movement.

◆ Children are learning to coordinate their vision with their body movements in order to step on the rope at just the right moment.

♦ When more than one child is playing at a time, the game encourages awareness of others in their space. Bumping into others gives them the clear tactile awareness that one space cannot be shared.

MODIFICATIONS

♦ For the child who has difficulty following the movements, start by encouraging her to step on the rope as it moves forward in a predictable slow movement.

CHAPTER 4

Social Fine Motor Games

Bingo Game

At last, a bingo game where no one dreads someone yelling, "Bingo!" because everyone wins.

GOALS

Increasing fine motor skills

Focusing

Eye-hand coordination

Visual stimulation

Awareness of others

MATERIALS

Colored construction paper

Poster board or cardboard

Poker chips or Styrofoam packing peanuts, cut-up pieces of cardboard, or any material of a similar size to be used as markers

SETUP

Make bingo cards by cutting a long, thin rectangle out of heavy cardboard or poster board around 12 × 4 inches. Paste four or five shapes, such as circle, triangle, square, star, and heart, on each card. Make each shape the same color, and place the same shapes on each card, but in a different order. Make an extra set of shapes as demonstration models.

DIRECTIONS

Have the children sit at a table and give each player a card. Have a leader hold up one of the demonstration cards, point to a shape, name it, and encourage the players to say the name and find the same shape on their own cards. When they have found the shape, they should cover it with a marker. Continue to hold up each shape until each child has each shape covered with a marker. Point out the success of each choice, even if assisted, "You found the circle; you found the same shape!"

When all of the shapes have been covered, everyone gets to say, "Bingo!"

VARIATIONS

1. Use circles of different colors instead of different shapes to teach color matching.

2. Use numbers for number recognition. Children have to put one marker on the number 1, two markers on the number 2, and so on.

WHAT IS BEING LEARNED

♦ Children are learning to follow a two-part direction. They need to first find the correct shape and then place a marker on it.

♦ The activity gives children more experience in matching, which can be expanded to include color, number, and letter recognition.

MODIFICATIONS

♦ Children who have difficulty looking at an object at a distance and then finding the match nearby will do better if the demonstration shape is held next to each shape on their board. For example, holding the heart shape next to the square shape, ask, "Is this the same?"

♦ Adding a tactile sensory component, such as making the shapes out of heavy cardboard so they can be felt as well as seen, can also be helpful for children who need more tactile than visual input.

Bubble Blowing

Take out a bubble wand, a jar of bubbles, and blow—and every kid (and grown-up) is captivated. In this game, the children can make all the bubbles they want with just a straw and some soapy water and then see those bubbles form designs on paper.

GOALS

Breath control
Working in a group
Realizing consequences of actions
Visual stimulation

MATERIALS

Bowl
Dish detergent
Food coloring
Straws

SETUP

Fill a bowl halfway with water. Add two or three tablespoons of dish detergent and some food coloring. Place the bowl in the middle of a small table.
If inside the house, first put a plastic sheet over the table to keep it from
getting wet.

DIRECTIONS

Have the children sit around the table so that they can all reach the bowl
with the straw when they lean in. Give each child a straw to place in the
bowl and have the children blow bubbles in the water. When a large amount
of bubbles are on top of the water, place a sheet of white or colored construction paper on top of the bubbles. The bubbles will pop on the paper,
making a beautiful circular design.

To prevent a child from sucking the bubble solution up the straw, poke
a few small holes in the straw one inch from the top.

VARIATIONS

1. Use an eggbeater instead of straws and have each child take a turn
   using it.

2. Use the paper to form cards that the children can draw or scribble on
   and give to parents.

3. Scoop up some bubbles and place them on your chin to make a
   "beard."

4. Scoop up some bubbles and place them on the table. Lightly blow on
   the top bubble and watch it expand.

WHAT IS BEING LEARNED

♦ Children are learning breath control. The harder they blow, the more bubbles they will get. They see the consequences of actions when they make the bubbles and when they see what happens when the paper is placed on the bubbles.

♦ They are all doing the same thing together. Being aware of this adds to the feeling of fun. Encourage this by saying, "Everyone is making bubbles. Let's all make even more!"

MODIFICATIONS

♦ For the child who cannot sustain an interest in blowing, have him help put the paper on top and see the results.

Cereal Box Puzzles

Cereal and cracker boxes can be used to make an instant puzzle. This is a good way to recycle, reuse, and educate.

GOALS

Noticing parts of a whole
Visual stimulation
Spatial awareness
Increasing fine motor control

MATERIALS

Cereal boxes
Scissors

SETUP

Cut out the front and back of the cereal box. Cut each side in half, forming two large rectangles.

Make a few sets of puzzles so each child in the group can have his own.

DIRECTIONS

Show children how the two parts can be put together to make a whole picture again. Then let them try it on their own. Provide assistance as needed. Once the children accomplish the task a few times, have them trade puzzles with another child.

VARIATIONS

1. After the children have mastered this game, you can cut or have them cut the halves in half again so that there are now four pieces to each puzzle.

2. Cut another box side with a diagonal cut this time so that you have two triangular halves instead of two rectangles.

3. When the children are ready for an added challenge, cut the pieces in abstract shapes rather than just squares, triangles, or rectangles. If your child needs help with this type of puzzle, you can lay the puzzle on a piece of paper and outline each piece so he can see more clearly how the shapes fit together.

4. You can also make a more attractive (and less commercial-looking) puzzle by pasting a picture from a magazine on a piece of cardboard instead. Pictures from *National Geographic* or *Smithsonian* magazines work well.

5. If you want to reuse the puzzles, they keep nicely in a brown mailing envelope. Or poke a hole in the corner of each puzzle piece, stick a paper clip through the holes, and hang them up on a cup hook.

WHAT IS BEING LEARNED

♦ Puzzles encourage children to notice similarities, such as how the color red or the bold line in one piece match up to the same features in another piece.

♦ When children try more than one puzzle, they are learning to transfer their knowledge from one experience to a similar one.

♦ By trading puzzles with classmates, they are learning the upside of sharing: that it enlarges your experience. In other words, if you share, then you get more puzzles.

MODIFICATIONS

♦ For children who have motoric difficulties and tend to be clumsy with their hands, lay down a nonslip mat so the cardboard puzzle pieces will stay put while the other piece or pieces are being added.

♦ To help children understand the concept of putting parts together to make a whole, make sure that they are part of the process by either letting them see the picture on the whole side of the box before you cut it, letting them help you cut the box, or letting them cut the box in half themselves.

Cereal Necklace

Art can be beautiful and art can be functional, but isn't it nice when it's also edible?

GOALS

Increasing fine motor skills

Focusing

Eye-hand coordination

Visual and proprioceptive stimulation

MATERIALS

Yarn, string, or fishing line
Cereal that has holes in the middle
Optional: tape

SETUP

Give each child a piece of yarn, string, or fishing line that is long enough to fit over her head when tied. If you use yarn or string, it can be helpful to younger ones if you put a piece of tape on the stringing end so that it's firmer and goes more easily through the hole in the cereal.

DIRECTIONS

Encourage the child to put the cereal pieces on the string. Give whatever assistance is needed to be successful. Tie the ends of the yarn together when she's done to make a necklace. Have your child count how many pieces of cereal are on the string.

VARIATIONS

1. After the child counts the number of cereal pieces on the string, let him eat some and then count how many pieces are left. Can your child figure out how many were eaten?

2. If you want your necklace to be lasting, instead of edible, string other things, such as buttons, short pieces of colored straws, or macaroni and other hollow pasta shapes.

3. Instead of string or yarn, you could use pipe cleaners and turn the project into rings for the fingers or loops to hang around the ears.

WHAT IS BEING LEARNED

♦ Children are getting practice in focusing on small objects and directing their fingers. They are also getting practice in counting and, for some, the concept of subtraction.

MODIFICATIONS

♦ For children who are not yet able to coordinate both hands working together, have an adult or other player hold the string steady.

Colored Slots

It takes a variety of methods to learn colors. This way encourages dexterity and socializing as well.

GOALS

Turn taking
Focusing
Eye-hand coordination
Matching

MATERIALS

Can with plastic lid (such as a coffee can)
Colored construction paper in four different colors
Tape
Scissors

SETUP

Make four slits in the plastic lid of a coffee can.

Tape a piece of different colored paper above each slit in the lid (see illustration).

Cut sheets of construction paper in the corresponding colors into small slips that will fit into the slits in the lid.

DIRECTIONS

Show children how to put the slips of paper into the slits that have the matching color above it. Once the game is learned or almost learned, encourage children to play the game together, taking turns putting the slips of paper into the correct slits.

VARIATIONS

1. Add more variations in color or more subtle differences in shade between the colors for the children who are already good at matching primary colors.

2. Play a similar game using shapes rather than colors.

3. Use playing cards and have larger slots labeled as hearts, diamonds, clubs, and spades.

WHAT IS BEING LEARNED

♦ Children are learning how to match colors (or shapes or patterns).

♦ If children play the game together, they are also learning how to wait for their turns and to be aware of another.

MODIFICATIONS

♦ If the child has trouble playing with another child, you can take the place of the other child until they are ready.

♦ For the child who needs more structure, do not put the paper in a pile within easy reach, but instead hand the papers out one by one to each child as he takes his turn. This will prevent one child from grabbing them all up and not taking turns.

Drawing Faces

The world is full of happy faces, but some children have difficulty reading expressions. By drawing smiling faces and other simple versions of emotions, we can open awareness to feelings.

GOALS

Awareness of emotion
Fine motor skills
Practicing reading facial expressions

MATERIALS

Paper
Pens

SETUP

Have one adult working with each child.

DIRECTIONS

Use one piece of paper per adult-child pair. Give each person a pen. The adult in each pair should draw a basic smiley face. Say, "A happy face" and smile at the child. The child should be encouraged to copy the adult's drawing, facial expression, or both.

Make a new drawing, but this time with a turned-down mouth to show a frown, and add tears to the eyes. Say, "A sad face" and make a sad face. Again, encourage imitation. Continue by drawing other basic facial expressions, such as a jagged mouth indicating a scared face and a flat mouth indicating an "OK" face.

VARIATIONS

1. Add variations to the eyebrows. For example, high or slanted inward for scared and slanted outward for sad.

2. Add body language to these expressions. Ask the children to guess which emotion you are feeling by your posture. Ask the children to take turns modeling a posture for others to identify.

WHAT IS BEING LEARNED

♦ Children are learning how to read facial expressions and body language so that they can better understand social cues.

♦ By drawing and seeing a drawing of a facial expression, they are able to identify the difference in mouth positions and, if doing the variation, the eyebrow positions.

MODIFICATIONS

♦ For children who do not yet have the hand control to draw, do a hand-over-hand drawing with them so they can feel what motions are used to draw these lines.

♦ Exaggerate the expressions to make them more apparent to the child who cannot yet read facial expressions.

♦ For children who seem oblivious to the different expressions, give added sensory or tactile input on the differences; encourage them to feel your sad (happy, scared, OK) face with their fingers.

Dump and Fill

Enjoying filling and dumping out objects is a stage in every child's development. In this game it's the filling step that is the changing challenge.

GOALS

Eye-hand coordination

Fine motor skills

Tactile and proprioceptive stimulation

Turn taking

MATERIALS

Marbles and a coffee can

or

Cut-up straws and a water bottle

or

Poker chips and a yogurt container

SETUP

If you use a coffee can, cut a hole in the plastic top that is slightly smaller than the marbles.

If you use a yogurt container, cut a slit in the top to fit the poker chip.

If you use a water bottle, remove the lid or make a tiny hole in the lid.

DIRECTIONS

Have two children play this game together, or an adult can play with a child. One person hands a marble to the one with the coffee can, who has to push the marble into the hole until it falls through to the can, making a satisfying *thunk*.

Let the children take turns being the one who puts the marble, straw, or poker chip into the appropriate container and the one who hands it to him. They also take turns dumping the container to start over.

VARIATIONS

1. Put all three choices in front of the child so he has to select the correct container for the object he is handed.

2. Have the child do the game with eyes blindfolded.

WHAT IS BEING LEARNED

♦ Children are learning to take turns and be a source of fun for each other.

♦ They are learning the basics of fine motor control, as it takes a pincer grasp to hold the objects, as well as eye-hand coordination in order to get the item in the hole.

♦ Because the hole for the marble is a little small, they are practicing their finger strength and their ability to move past a little frustration to success.

MODIFICATIONS

♦ If your player is likely to put objects in his mouth, don't use the marble game, but do use the poker chips and make the straw pieces too big to swallow.

♦ If your player is not ready for the fine motor aspects, remove the tops of the containers and let him just put it in and dump it out without the additional challenge.

Eyedropper Squirts

Here is a game that has three important elements. It takes fine motor skills to work the eyedropper, cognitive skills to understand the principle of fill and release, and a sense of fun to squirt another.

GOALS

Playfulness
Awareness of others
Fine motor control
Cognition of a two-step process
Tactile stimulation

MATERIALS

One eyedropper per child

Pail of water or a smaller container of water for each child

SETUP

Give each child an eyedropper and a separate container of water, or put the one pail of water in the middle of a circle for them all to share.

DIRECTIONS

Show each child how to fill the eyedropper with water by using a four-part sequence:

First, squeeze the top closed.

Second, place the eyedropper in the water.

Third, stop squeezing the top of the eyedropper and watch the water come up the tube.

Fourth, take it out of the water, squeeze the top again, and squirt the water (on each other!).

VARIATIONS

1. Squirt water on specific body parts, as in "Let's squirt water on my (or your) hand. Now on your elbow."

2. Use paints instead of water and squirt paint on paper. Have different colors in separate eyedroppers or clear the eyedropper with water between colors.

3. Using paint, drop paint from higher and higher distances to get different effects in the paint splotches on paper.

WHAT IS BEING LEARNED

◆ By squirting water at each other, children are becoming more aware of each other and enjoying the silly give-and-take of the situation. They also gain experience in motor planning as they modify the squirt to aim it up and out and connect with the person they are aiming at!

- ◆ If they squirt their different body parts, they are increasing their awareness of the parts of their bodies and the names of those parts.

- ◆ If they drop paint from the dropper onto paper they get the fun of experimenting with color. They get to see how different colors look next to each other and how the paint forms a different design when dropped from higher distances.

MODIFICATIONS

- ◆ Tactilely defensive children might have difficulty with a sudden burst of water squirted out. Instead, dribble the water slowly on different body parts to help increase their tolerance.

- ◆ If the child can't handle that amount of touch yet, you can both squirt water at something else, such as at your reflections in the mirror.

Feather Blowing

Watching feathers can be fascinating because they move slowly and respond to the slightest current.

GOALS

Eye-hand coordination
Partner play
Breath control and modulation
Visual, proprioceptive, and vestibular input

MATERIALS

Small feathers

SETUP

If two children play together, have them stand close, facing each other. If it's an adult and a child, the adult should be at the child's level.

DIRECTIONS

Show your partner how to cup her hands in anticipation of catching a floating feather. Softly blow a feather and have your partner catch it. Give as little or as much help as is needed.

Take turns being the blower and the catcher.

Work toward having two children play together, with adults assisting as needed.

VARIATIONS

1. Get in a circle and blow the feather from one person to the next.

2. Have each child blow a feather up and catch it with his own hands.

3. Use a balloon instead of a feather. Or blow up the balloon, then let it go, and have the child try to catch it as it flies around the room.

WHAT IS BEING LEARNED

♦ Children are learning to modulate their breath, which controls volume. They need to know how to control their breath so they can learn to use their "inside voices." Controlled respiration also helps create longer sentences.

♦ Controlled breathing also helps create calmness.

♦ They are practicing focusing because they have to keep their eyes on the feather in order to catch it. And they have to get their hands in position to catch the falling feather. Thus, they are learning eye-hand coordination.

♦ If the children have to move in order to get in the best position to catch the feather, they are challenging their sense of balance and thereby increasing it.

♦ They are also learning the pleasures of back-and-forth play.

MODIFICATIONS

♦ For the child who gets distracted more easily and won't keep his eye on the feather, make the distance between you very small and reward him

for each catch. The reward can be whatever he likes, such as a hug, high five, treat, favorite toy, or verbal praise.

- ◆ For children who need more work on breath control, which is an underlying factor in the ability to speak longer sentences, hold the feather in your hand and have them practice blowing softly and then blowing strongly. Comment on the difference.
- ◆ For children who need a lot of visual stimulation in order to stay attentive, use the balloon variation.

Listening Game

Hearing a sound they can't identify can be scary for children, and there are so many sounds in our world. This game helps make them familiar.

GOALS

Listening
Identifying
Auditory stimulation
Group participation

MATERIALS

Recording of common sounds

SETUP

Make a recording of common sounds, such as a car starting, water running, a vacuum cleaner running, a dog barking, a door closing, and a toilet flushing.

DIRECTIONS

Have the children sit and tell them you are going to ask them to listen to some sounds. When they are quiet, start the recording. Stop the recording after each sound and ask, "What made that sound?" If needed, give them choices, "Was that a toilet flushing or a dog barking?" Make the choices as obvious or subtle as needed by your group.

VARIATIONS

1. Let one of the players start and stop the recorder.

2. Have children try to imitate the sounds they hear.

WHAT IS BEING LEARNED

♦ Children are learning to identify by sound the things that are in their lives. This will help them not be alarmed when a sound comes on suddenly. They begin to see that many things make a sound and these sounds can be identified.

♦ They are also being part of a group and hearing others' interpretations.

MODIFICATIONS

♦ For the child who alarms easily, let him control the stopping and starting of the recorder, or play the sounds at a low volume.

♦ For the child who needs visuals to understand, have photos or pictures of the objects to accompany the sounds.

Lost in Rice

This is a classic game, and there is a reason for that. Everyone enjoys digging for treasures.

GOALS

Playing with others
Tactile stimulation
Decreasing tactile sensitivity

MATERIALS

Rice or any small, dry material, such as beans, birdseed, corn kernels,
and so on
Medium-size container or bucket
Small toys or objects, such as toy cars, figures, wrapped treats, combs,
Ping-Pong balls, and so on

SETUP

Fill a container with the rice or other material. Use a basin, box, or any
container that allows children the freedom to dig without the rice spilling
over the sides.

DIRECTIONS

Either bury the items in the rice yourself, or have another child bury the
items to find. You can do this with or without the child watching.

"Tanya buried something in the rice. Can you find it? A car! You found
a car!"

Let the child play with the car for a while before saying, "Now it's your
turn to bury the car for Tanya to find."

VARIATIONS

1. For a small number of children, bury quite a few toys in the rice and
   have each child take a turn to find an object.

2. Name one of the objects hidden and encourage children to find the
   object without looking and using just their hands.

WHAT IS BEING LEARNED

♦ If children watch the toy being buried, they learn that objects that are
no longer seen still exist (object permanence). If they have tactile issues,

they can learn to increase their tolerance. If they tend to put things in their mouths to identify texture, they learn to use their finger pads for identification instead.

♦ Feeling the pressure of the rice or other material on their hands as they search for the toys can also be very calming.

MODIFICATIONS

♦ For the child who is tactilely sensitive and reluctant to let his hands touch unfamiliar things, allow him to watch the desired toy being buried so that he'll be willing to go get it. As he becomes more familiar and comfortable with the game, try using other materials, such as sand or damp oatmeal, to get him to tolerate more textures. Keep a bucket of water nearby so he can rinse as needed. Then, later, keep the bucket of water further away so he learns to tolerate the feeling for longer periods.

Penny Flick

This is a quickly organized social and fine motor game with an easy-to-find material, pennies.

GOALS

Playing with others
Visual focusing
Eye-hand coordination
Fine motor control

MATERIALS

Pennies (or poker chips, quarters, bottle caps)

SETUP

Partner two children across from each other or have children sitting around a circular table.

DIRECTIONS

Give the children each a penny and show how to move the pennies along the table by flicking their index finger with their thumb or by pushing with just their index finger or the side of their thumb. They can use whatever finger method works best for them (the method doesn't matter).

If you do the partner game, have the players sitting across from each other flick their pennies toward each other, trying to get them to touch.

If you use the group game, have all the players flick their pennies into the center of the table and try to get the pennies to bump into each other.

VARIATIONS

1. Set up two objects, such as two cups or just two other pennies, a short distance away from the flickers to serve as "goal posts." The players have to flick their pennies between the two objects. Keep making the "goal posts" closer together to increase the challenge.

2. Use straws, spoon handles, tongue depressors, or popsicle or craft sticks as hockey sticks, call the penny a "puck," and bat the puck back and forth between the players.

3. Make a line of pennies and have the player try and hit each penny and knock it out of line.

4. Make a line of pennies with at least an inch of space between them and have the player try to flick his penny through each of the spaces. Make the first space the largest and each following space progressively smaller.

5. Show children how to place a penny on its edge, give it a little push, and watch it roll. See how far it can go without falling over.

WHAT IS BEING LEARNED

♦ Children are engaged in back-and-forth play in which they are either taking turns or playing simultaneously.

♦ The small muscles of the hand are getting a workout in this game, and children are learning how to grade the energy output of those muscles to produce the desired results.

MODIFICATIONS

♦ Children who have dif-
   ficulty controlling their
   fingers would do better
   if they used the second
   variation of a "hockey
   stick."

♦ If the child might put
   small objects in his
   mouth, use objects too
   big to swallow, such as
   poker chips, quarters, or
   large bottle caps.

Point to the Cup

Learning to point and, even more important, learning to understand what pointing means, can be a tricky skill for young children with ASD.

GOALS

Pointing as communication
Visual stimulation
Naming objects

MATERIALS

Three plastic or paper cups
Small objects—little plastic figures or other common objects, such as
   coins, rings, bells, and so on

SETUP

Place the three cups upside down on the table.

DIRECTIONS

In view of the child, put an object, such as an animal figure, under one of the cups. Ask, "Where is the bear? Is it here?" (Model pointing to one cup.) "Or here?" (Point to another cup.) "Or here?" (Point to the third cup.) Encourage the child to point to the correct cup using hand-over-hand prompting if needed.

Keep the cups out of reach to discourage grabbing for the object. The second the child points or attempts to point at the correct cup, immediately reward her by giving her the object.

If the child reaches, rather than points, for the correct cup, pretend ignorance and lift the wrong cup, asking again for a pointing response.

VARIATIONS

1. Use more than three cups to enlarge choices or only one to reduce choice.

2. Instead of cups, hide an object or objects around the room and ask the child to point to where the bear is hiding, for example.

WHAT IS BEING LEARNED

♦ Children are learning to communicate their wants. For nonverbal children, it's frustrating to want something and not be able to communicate that need. Pointing is a first step.

♦ Pointing is one of the first communication skills and can be easier to learn than following an eye gaze. The basic idea for these games is to make pointing interesting and useful. You also want the child to understand that pointing is used in different ways and in combination with different words.

MODIFICATIONS

♦ To help children learn to point, first place objects on the table and have children touch each object with their index finger as they are named.

This helps children understand that a pointed finger directs attention across a distance.

♦ To keep a child interested in the game, put one of his favorite objects that he wants under the cup.

♦ To help children be very clear about their pointing, place the cups at a distance from each other so that pointing to the left is very different from pointing to the right.

Pudding Party

Messy fun is a good way to help children see the joy in getting dirty.

GOALS

Decreasing tactile defensiveness
Increasing tactile awareness
Fine motor control

MATERIALS

Pudding, yogurt, or any ready-made whipped topping
Plastic sheet
Aprons (or garbage bags with holes for head and arms to be used as
    aprons)
Optional: food coloring

SETUP

Cover a table with a plastic sheet and cover the children with aprons or modified garbage bags. If you want, add food coloring to the pudding or other food to make it different colors.

DIRECTIONS

Help children spoon a blob of pudding in front of them and use their hands to spread the goop.

Demonstrate how to write or make marks in the pudding. For example, draw circles of the first letter of their names.

Use fingers, cotton swabs, toothpicks, paintbrushes, or combs to get different effects.

VARIATIONS

1. Use dry materials, such as cornmeal, birdseed, sand, or talcum powder, depending on the likelihood that children will put the substance in their mouths.

2. Use wet sand or shaving cream if the children are not likely to put it in their mouths.

3. Place a mirror under the substance so children can see their reflections when they swish the material around.

4. Let children put their feet in shaving cream by placing it on a tray or cookie sheet on the floor.

WHAT IS BEING LEARNED

♦ Children are learning to tolerate touching goopy material. They are also getting an opportunity to isolate their pointer fingers, increasing their dexterity, and to practice making purposeful marks.

MODIFICATIONS

♦ For children who find it too difficult to touch these materials, give them thick plastic gloves or thicker kitchen gloves to wear, or use dry substances, such as powder or cornstarch.

♦ Let children use a paintbrush or stick for exploring until they are ready to try using their hands.

Secret Message

Watching something appear from nothing feeds a child's delight in magic.

GOALS

Increasing fine motor skills

Focusing

Increasing attention span
Visual and proprioceptive stimulation
Increasing language skills

MATERIALS

Heavy white paper, such as index cards
Candle
Paints and brushes or paint bottles with sponge tops

SETUP

Using the candle, draw simple shapes or pictures on white index cards

DIRECTIONS

Give each child one of the index cards. Encourage children to paint over the paper and see the shape or figure that appears on the card. Ask them to say the name of the shape or figure they see.

VARIATIONS

1. Write letters instead of drawing shapes or figures. Do a card for each letter of the child's name and then encourage him to put them in the right order to spell his name.

2. Have the children draw pictures and shapes on the cards and give them to each other.

WHAT IS BEING LEARNED

♦ Children learn to do an action and anticipate a result. When they paint on the card, something will appear.

♦ If the variation is used in which the children give each other cards, they practice a social give-and-take.

MODIFICATIONS

♦ For children who need more input on drawing the shapes themselves, use colored crayons instead of candles so they can see what they have drawn. The paint, put on by another player, will make the shape stand out more.

♦ For children who do not have the fine motor control to use a paintbrush, use bottled paint that has a sponge applicator that will cover large areas more easily.

Sink the Boat

This game has an element of suspense. Will your pebble be the one that sinks the boat? Watch and see.

GOALS

Working with others to achieve a common goal
Eye-hand coordination
Visual and proprioceptive stimulation
Understanding of cause and effect

MATERIALS

Plastic basin (like the kind used for dishwashing)
Pebbles
Small plastic container (such as a margarine container) or Styrofoam meat tray

SETUP

Place a basin in the middle of the table, filled with water.

Float a small plastic container (or tray) on the water.

DIRECTIONS

Tell the players that they are going to see how many pebbles it takes to sink the boat. Go around the table giving each child in turn a pebble and have them put their pebble in the small container.

Comment on the progress. After one child puts his pebble in, say, "Still floating. Next turn," "Still floating," and so on until, "It sank!"

VARIATIONS

1. Have several containers floating on the water to be sunk, one at a time.

2. Play the "Will it sink or float?" game instead. Take turns placing various objects, such a feather, cork, rock, penny, and so forth, on the water to see if they will sink or float.

WHAT IS BEING LEARNED

♦ Because all of the children are contributing, the success of the boat sinking has the potential of making a child feel a part of the whole group, an often unusual but welcome experience for the child who wants to interact with others but is unsure how to do so.

♦ If children toss the pebble into the container rather than just placing it in, there is the possibility of increasing their eye-hand coordination.

♦ If you do the variation of several boats, you can use this activity to practice counting. How many boats sank?

MODIFICATIONS

♦ Practice ahead of time, on your own, to see how many pebbles it takes to sink the boat. Vary the size of the pebbles or the size of the boat to fit the attention span of your group. If they would get too impatient or distracted and lose the connection between their actions and the consequence, use a smaller container or larger pebbles.

♦ If you're worried that some kids will throw their pebbles while waiting their turns, give each child a pebble at the moment it's her turn, rather than handing out the pebbles ahead of time.

♦ If your child is likely to put pebbles in his mouth, use larger objects, such as small rocks that are too big to be swallowed. The boat will just sink a little faster.

Smelling Game

This game is a good way to find out what smells kids avoid and which they prefer, and it also stimulates their olfactory sense.

GOALS

Olfactory stimulation
Turn taking

MATERIALS

Clean, empty plastic pill containers
Cotton balls
Variety of substances to smell, such as peanut butter, maple syrup, roses, coffee, lemon, vanilla, peppermint, garlic, onions, pepper

SETUP

Put a small amount of each substance in a medicine bottle. Put a hole in the lid of each container. If the substance is liquid, first put a dab on a cotton ball and put the cotton ball in the container.

Have the children sit in a circle or at a table.

DIRECTIONS

Demonstrate how to strongly inhale over the hole of the lid. Pass the container around, and have the children guess the smell and say if they like it

or not. Assign one child to pass the container from child to child. Give each
child a chance to be that person.

VARIATIONS

1. Give children three or more containers at a time and ask them to find a
   specific aroma.

2. Have children make their own containers with different substances.

WHAT IS BEING LEARNED

♦ Children are learning to identify smells. They are becoming aware that
  smells have particular sources so that they can more clearly identify
  their preferences or dislikes.

♦ Roses and vanilla are generally considered calming, whereas peppermint and lemon are invigorating. If your child discovers an aroma that
  is calming, he learns to seek it out when needing calmness.

♦ The child who gets to pass the containers around experiences being the
  important leader and being aware of each child's reaction.

MODIFICATIONS

♦ Start with easy, pleasant odors for the child who is defensive, and then
  work toward stronger ones. For example, start with the roses and work
  your way up to the onions. If a child has an aversion to smelling the containers, let her be the one who hands the containers to others instead, if
  she's willing.

♦ Rather than have them identify the name of the smell, talk about when
  or where they smelled that before. For example, a coffee smell might
  remind them of mornings and vanilla might remind them of cookies.

Sound Makers

*Along with learning to imitate and make sounds, it's good to know that
everything can make music. Kids have a great time with this game inspired*

by the Broadway show "Stomp," which features music and dance with trash-can lids.

GOALS

Listening
Rhythm
Group play
Understanding of cause and effect
Auditory stimulation

MATERIALS

Household items that make sounds, such as an eggbeater, wooden
spoons, pot lid and spoon, chopsticks, timers with ringers, alarm
clock, bell, keys on a ring, grater and spoon

SETUP

Put a variety of the above materials in one container. Have the children sit
in a circle or in a small group.

DIRECTIONS

Pass the objects out to the children or let them choose their own. Let children experiment with making sounds with their "instruments." The instruments can be played all at the same time, or each one can be passed around the circle so that all of the children have experience with that instrument.

VARIATIONS

1. Add spontaneous vocal sounds and a rhythmic beat to the playing.
   Encourage children to imitate the sounds and rhythms.

2. Sing a familiar song, such as "Twinkle, Twinkle, Little Star," and encourage the children to bang on their instruments in a similar rhythm.

3. Make homemade sound shakers by filling yogurt cups or plastic water bottles with different household objects, such as rice, beans, salt, sand, birdseed, coins, beads, pebbles, and so on.

WHAT IS BEING LEARNED

♦ Children are learning to do activities with others and to be aware of being part of a group activity.

♦ When adding vocals to the sound, they are being introduced to the idea of making music out of whatever is around, and are starting to get the sense of rhythm and keeping a beat.

♦ There is also a feeling of joy that can come from banging pot lids together and making other simple sounds.

♦ Children who figure out how to make an alarm clock or timer ring are also gaining an understanding of cause and effect and how to make things work.

MODIFICATIONS

♦ For children who are hypersensitive to sounds, work with them individually on playing softly and experimenting with increasingly louder sounds.

♦ For children who have difficulty with sensory modulation, help them experience the difference between banging lids with full intensity and tapping them softly. The repetition and variation of this activity helps them to explore and modify their responses.

Straw Sucking

Speech requires the ability to control the muscles of the lips, tongue, and throat, which are all developed in the act of sucking on something. In this game children get an unusual way to practice the art of sucking.

GOALS

Oral control
Following direction
Modulation

MATERIALS

Stickers
One straw per child
Piece of paper

SETUP

Lay the stickers out on a table.

DIRECTIONS

Demonstrate how to suck on a straw to get the sticker to adhere to the bottom of the straw. Then release the sticker by stopping sucking in the air.

Ask a child to practice picking up the sticker with the straw and dropping it into your hand. In this way you can have your hand in the right place until his control is better.

Next lay out a series of stickers and ask the child to move a particular one to a separate piece of paper.

VARIATIONS

1. Once all the stickers are moved, have the child peel off the backs and stick the stickers onto the paper.

2. Instead of stickers, use heavier objects, such as pictures on construction paper. This requires increased breath control.

WHAT IS BEING LEARNED

◆ Children are learning oral and breath control and how to modulate this control so that the sticker stays connected to the straw or is purposely released.

♦ They are experiencing listening to and following directions and, if they use the variation of peeling off the stickers, they are getting some fine motor experience as well.

MODIFICATIONS

♦ For children who are having a hard time understanding sucking, have them start with blowing through the straw at objects that move easily when blown, such as cotton balls. Using sound, exaggerate the difference between blowing out and sucking in, and encourage the child to suck in and get the cotton ball to adhere to the straw.

Styrofoam Hammering

Styrofoam blocks provide just the right amount of resistance to hold a golf tee upright but respond immediately to any hammer blows, so the beginner only has to hammer lightly to see results.

GOALS

Playing with others
Eye-hand coordination
Proprioceptive stimulation
Tactile stimulation
Increasing strength

MATERIALS

Styrofoam block, such as from packing material
Small hammer or rock
Golf tees

SETUP

Take a block of Styrofoam and press in the tips of golf tees so that the head of the tee and most of its length protrudes. Place the tees two to three inches apart.

DIRECTIONS

Give a child a small toy wooden hammer, or a tack hammer, or any hammer you feel comfortable with him using. Or, if you don't have an appropriate hammer, you can use a rock.

Show him how to hammer the tee into the block.

Show him how he can pull the hammered tees back out of the Styrofoam, place them in another unused area of the block, and hammer again.

Once the process is learned, have the children take turns or have one child hand the tees to the other to pound. Or have the children take turns being the one who hammers and the one who pulls the tees out.

VARIATIONS

1. Use screws and a screwdriver.

2. Don't use a hammer, but have children press the tee in with their fingers.

3. Use flat-top roofing nails instead of golf tees.

WHAT IS BEING LEARNED

♦ There's nothing like hammering to hammer home the concept of eye-hand coordination. To be effective, you have to watch what you are doing!

♦ Children get the experience of being part of another's project by handing them the next tee.

MODIFICATIONS

♦ Children who have difficulty sharing and taking turns might need to start this game by playing alone until they have had a satisfactory amount of turns. Once the novelty wears off, they might be more willing to take turns.

♦ Using the variation of pushing the tees in with their hands will work better for children who do not yet have the eye-hand coordination to aim the hammer. If you use this method, place the tee in an already made hole so that it slips down more easily.

~ ~ ~ ~ ~ ~ ~ ~ ~ ~ ~ ~ ~ ~ ~ ~ ~ ~ ~ ~

Tile Painting

Painting on a tile instead of on paper means you'll never run out of a painting surface. A tissue immediately wipes away the last drawing and makes it ready for the next. Also, the smoothness of the tile's surface provides ease in drawing.

GOALS

Encouraging creativity
Increasing fine motor control
Awareness of others

MATERIALS

Plain white or lightly colored tiles, any size
Colored felt-tip pens or paints
Damp paper towel, sponge, or tissue

SETUP

Give each person a piece of tile and place a variety of colored markers in the center of the table for everyone to choose from.

DIRECTIONS

Let the children draw whatever they want on the tile and have them watch you do the same. When the pictures are done, make a point of holding up each person's tile so everyone can see the work. Make appropriate praising comments, even if they are very simple, such as "Reggie's tile has lots of red in it. Red is a fun color."

Show children how to use a tissue, sponge, or paper towel to wipe off the design when finished.

VARIATIONS

1. Draw lines and have children copy your designs. For beginners, start with horizontal and vertical lines and circles. Work toward crosses, x's, squares, and rectangles.

2. Let the child lead and copy whatever marks he makes. "I'm going to make a squiggle like yours." Take turns leading and following.

3. Turn simple lines into drawings, such as making a circle and a vertical line into a balloon with a string.

WHAT IS BEING LEARNED

♦ Children are experimenting with making art on a new type of surface, as well as learning how to erase and redo.

♦ They are noticing what others are doing and seeing variations using the same materials.

♦ Mainly, they are experiencing the joy of creating.

MODIFICATIONS

♦ If you have a child who tends to throw things as a way of showing she is finished with the project, you may want to use linoleum tiles instead of ceramic.

♦ For the child who needs things to be organized in order not to get distracted, use a small tray and put the tile and one or two pens on the tray so that his materials are all in one place.

♦ If your children are more advanced and would like to work on perfecting the drawing, use the corner of a paper towel or cotton swab to wipe away any part that they wish to redo.

♦ If they do want to save their artwork, make a color photocopy, or cover the tile with clear cellophane tape or clear contact paper.

Toothpick Treats

Here's a game that encourages focusing and fine motor development, and you get to eat a treat!

GOALS

Increasing fine motor skills

Focusing

Eye-hand coordination

Visual stimulation

MATERIALS

Toothpicks

Raisins

SETUP

Each child gets a toothpick. For the child who can work independently, place a little pile of raisins in front of him. For the child who needs assistance, have an adult or classmate hand him one raisin at a time.

DIRECTIONS

Demonstrate how to poke the toothpick through the raisins until the toothpick is full. Then the child can eat the raisins.

VARIATIONS

1. Make abstract sculptures or models of animals, people, buildings, or shapes.

2. Use cereal to place on toothpicks.

WHAT IS BEING LEARNED

◆ The children are getting a chance to practice coordinating the small muscles of their hands and focusing their attention on a task. There is a clear end to the project (when the toothpick is full) and the reward of eating the raisins.

MODIFICATIONS

♦ For the child who wants to eat each raisin, encourage him to alternate: one raisin for his mouth, one to go on the toothpick.

♦ If raisins have too much sugar for a hyperactive child, use lightly cooked dried peas instead.

♦ For children who crave oral input and need more chewing than raisins will provide, have a small dish of pretzels nearby for munching while spearing the raisins.

What's in the Sock?

Identifying objects with their eyes or fingers is a practical exercise in being aware of what's in one's environment.

GOALS

Increasing tactile awareness
Environmental awareness
Building vocabulary

MATERIALS

One clean sock
Variety of small common household objects, such as a pencil, coins,
orange, comb, hairbrush, glue bottle, spoon, fork, and carrot

SETUP

Place at least three objects in the sock without the children seeing.

DIRECTIONS

Put the objects inside a sock and have a child reach in and pull one out. Ask her to say the name of the object. If nonverbal, ask yes-no questions, such as "Is this a comb?" or questions that require saying a word, such as "Is this a comb or a spoon?"

If the child is more advanced, name an object that she needs to feel for and take out "Put your hand inside and find the coin."

VARIATIONS

1. Place only one object in the sock and ask your player to identify what is in the sock by just feeling the outside of the sock and not looking inside.

2. Allow children to gather objects from around the area and place them in the sock. Then the adult or another child can be the guesser.

WHAT IS BEING LEARNED

♦ On one level, children are developing their vocabulary as they learn the names of things in their surroundings.

♦ When feeling and guessing, the child is focusing on the information that her fingertips are sending, which her brain is receiving and identifying.

♦ When the child is the gatherer of objects, his attention is more open as he scans the environment for something that is just the right size and texture.

MODIFICATIONS

♦ For the child who is echolalic and would just repeat the last word if given a choice of two words, only say the name of the object to repeat.

♦ For the tactilely defensive child who is reluctant to put her hands into the unknown, put the objects in an open box and ask her to give you the objects named.

Yes-No Game

Teaching children to say "Yes" or "No" or to shake or nod their heads provides an important beginning communication skill. Because it is common for children with ASD to enjoy sorting objects according to color or size, we use this knowledge to teach them by incorporating a sense of humor and doing it purposely wrong!

GOALS

Improving communication
Developing sense of humor
Head control
Visual and auditory stimulation

MATERIALS

Sorting toy, such as a shape box, color sorter, or pole with colored rings

SETUP

Place the sorting toy on the table. Place the objects to be sorted next to it.

DIRECTIONS

Pick up one of the objects and purposely put it in the wrong place. Then say, "No!" which is probably what the child is thinking, and put it in the correct place, saying, "Yes!" Each time, combine the words with the physical action of shaking your head for "No" and nodding it for "Yes."

Continue with the other objects, each time doing an exaggerated "No" when you put it in the wrong place. If the child is already good at sorting, let her correct you and put it in the correct place while you say an affirming, "Yes!"

VARIATIONS

1. Use puzzles instead of sorting toys.

2. Make some mistakes even more ridiculous, such as putting socks on the child's fingers.

WHAT IS BEING LEARNED

♦ You are teaching the meaning of "No" and "Yes," both the verbal and the physical expression.

♦ If you do the silly variations, children can experience a fun interchange with each other.

MODIFICATIONS

♦ Very concrete thinkers may just think you're not very smart. Aim for being comical so children will learn that you are purposely being silly and will see the humor in the game.

CHAPTER 5

Water Games

Although the games in this chapter involve water, most of them can be played with just a water table, other water container, or a shallow kiddie pool. And many of the big pool games can be varied to play on land instead. If you want to play in a pool, but don't have a community, school, or backyard pool available, you might approach a hotel. Many allow outside guests pool privileges for a small fee.

Being surrounded by water instead of air provides a very special sensory experience. Water has a distinctive feel on the skin, and the even, hydrostatic pressure enveloping the body can be soothing and calming. Generally, warm water relaxes the body, while cooler water invigorates and activates it. Buoyancy creates a sense of weightless and freer motion while moving against the resistance of water proves wonderful sensory input. Best of all, water-based activity can be a fun, motivating way to improve sensory comfort, sensorimotor skills, and overall physical fitness.

—Lindsey Biel, MA, OTR/L and Nancy Peske, *Raising a Sensory Smart Child* (p. 47)

In the pleasing environment of gently lapping water, it is easier for children to respond socially because they are more relaxed. Aquatic therapy also has a practical result. Having children be comfortable and capable in the water is a smart skill, whether in a large body of water or in a kiddie pool. Kids need to be water friendly.

When playing around any water, you should always assign one adult to each child. If your program doesn't have enough adults on staff, encourage parents or interested adults to join the group. Always make sure children have adequate safety equipment. Things like inner tubes, rafts, and noodles are fun, but they can't take the place of life jackets. And never leave children unsupervised around any type of water. Children can drown in as little as a few inches of water. When first getting into the pool, start with a little "free time" before introducing the games. In this way, children get used to the temperature and novelty of being in the water. If there are several children and adults in a group, it's a good time to meet and greet and have simple interactions.

Blow Bubbles and Hum

Learning to put one's face in the water can be scary. Blowing bubbles and humming help distract from the fear.

GOALS

Oral control
Focusing
Tolerating having one's face in the water
Sensory discrimination input

MATERIALS

Shallow end of a pool, kiddie pool, or bathtub
Life jackets

SETUP

Have children and adults sit in the shallow water with their chins in the water.

DIRECTIONS

While your and the child's chins are in the water, exaggerate closing your mouth by first opening your mouth and then closing it. When you close your mouth, start to hum and slowly lower your mouth into the water while continuing to hum. Have the child copy what you are doing.

Next, open and close your mouth but, instead of humming, blow on the surface of the water and continue blowing as you lower your mouth into the water making bubbles. Again have the child copy what you do.

VARIATIONS

1. Once children are comfortable with putting their faces under the water, have them hum a specific tune while underwater, such as "Twinkle, Twinkle, Little Star."

2. Pretend to be motorboats and blow bubbles underwater while moving about.

WHAT IS BEING LEARNED

♦ Children are learning to be more accepting of having their faces underwater, a necessary prerequisite for swimming.

♦ They are learning to consciously control the muscles of their lips and jaws and noticing the difference between pursing their lips and keeping them closed, which are good oral motor skills for speech. They are also learning to control respiration and regulate their breathing.

MODIFICATIONS

♦ For children who are just learning to blow, have them start by blowing the water with a straw. Make a hole near the top of the straw so the water doesn't go in their mouths. If they can't do this, they can even start by blowing Ping-Pong balls on top of the surface of the water.

Boogie Board Ride

Boogie boards are too much fun to just use riding waves. Instead of waves, kids can ride in the pool.

GOALS

Alertness
Vestibular stimulation
Accepting a new experience

MATERIALS

Boogie board
Pool
Life jackets

SETUP

One or two adults hold the boogie board steady so that a child can be placed in a sitting position on top.

DIRECTIONS

When the child is sitting comfortably on the board, give him a ride around the pool, encouraging him to keep his balance. Adults can adjust the board so that the child does not fall in, or you can allow the child to experience the effectiveness of his own physical adjustments.

VARIATIONS

1. Have the child kneel or lie down instead of sitting.

2. Two or more children can sit together.

3. One child can hold onto the leash of the board and take another child for a ride, with an adult supervising and pointing out what is happening "Look, you are giving Chris a ride!"

WHAT IS BEING LEARNED

◆ Children are learning to maintain their balance on a moving surface. If successful at adjusting their balance with the movement, they are rewarded with a ride. If not, they get instant feedback and fall in the water. Some kids who love jumping into water will especially enjoy this part. They are experiencing doing something they probably have never done before, and that can be big fun.

◆ Children who pull the leash and give another a ride experience being responsible for another's fun.

MODIFICATIONS

◆ A child who has difficulty with balance or who has gravitational insecurity may do better lying on the board with an adult's arm securely holding him across his back, or with a hand on his back. This will make him feel safer and more willing to experiment with a moving surface.

Bury the Body

If you happen to be at the beach for your water games, this is always a good activity. Getting buried in the sand is not only fun for kids but also can be great therapy.

GOALS

Body awareness
Tactile stimulation
Achieving goals
Proprioceptive stimulation
Enlarging tactile tolerance

MATERIALS

Sandy beach

SETUP

The child is sitting on the sand.

DIRECTIONS

Have an adult or adults put increasing amounts of sand on a child's arms and legs while explaining what is being done, "I'm going to cover up your foot. Now your leg," and so on. Continue to cover as much of the body as the child seems to enjoy. Encourage other children to help.

After the child is covered and is ready to end the game, you could play-fully ask, "Where are your feet? I lost your feet! Oh, there they are!" Continue until the whole body reemerges.

VARIATIONS

1. Use wet sand instead of dry to increase the weight of the sand.

2. Make a hole for the child to sit in to increase the tactile input.

WHAT IS BEING LEARNED

♦ Being covered in the sand stimulates the body's tactile system and can increase alertness or, depending on the child's sensory system, can calm and settle the child, in the way that a heavy blanket can produce a calming feeling.

♦ The physical feedback from the weight of the sand increases awareness of body parts, especially if the body part is named while being covered.

MODIFICATIONS

♦ The adult saying, "I lost your foot," may alarm children who are concrete thinkers! The reappearance of the foot and the lightness of your tone might help him learn about less literal forms of thinking.

◆ Children who have tactile defensiveness and are reluctant or scared to allow their body parts to be covered may do better if they are the ones covering up someone else, rather than being covered themselves. Or start with a small, gentle version of this activity, such as only covering the toes or fingers, and have a pail of water nearby or sit near the ocean's edge so the child can rinse off whenever she wants. This will increase the sense of being in control.

◆ Do this game each time the child is at the beach. The consistency will increase familiarity and this predictability will make this tactile game more acceptable and enjoyable.

Catch a Fish

The novelty of this game makes it easy for children to attend, and the challenge is not too hard and not too easy.

GOALS

Focused attention
Joint attention
Imagination
Task completion
Eye-hand coordination
Motor planning

MATERIALS

Ping-Pong balls (paint eyes on them for added interest)
Small bowl or container (such as a large, empty plastic yogurt container)
Large bowl or bucket or water table
Small strainers or fishing nets

SETUP

Put the Ping-Pong ball "fishes" in a small bowl or container. Put water in the larger bowl or bucket. Have players sit in a circle around the bucket either independently or on an adult's lap. Give each player a strainer or fishing net.

DIRECTIONS

Show the children the container of Ping-Pong ball "fishes" and then dump them into the water saying, "Uh-oh, the fish got away. Help me catch them and put them back in the bowl." Demonstrate how to catch the fish with a strainer or fishing net and put it into the bowl. Encourage the children to catch fish with their strainers and empty them into the bowl. Continue doing this until all the fishes are back in the bowl.

Show the children that the bowl is filled again. Then pretend the fish got away again by turning the bowl over ("Oh no—they got away again!") and asking the group to gather them back up.

Sing a song that would go with the game, such as this one to the tune of "Catch a Falling Star":

Catch a little fish and put it in the bowl and never let it get away

VARIATIONS

1. Use other things that float, such as packing peanuts, rubber miniature dolls, or corks.

2. Use tongs to pick up the fish instead of strainers.

WHAT IS BEING LEARNED

♦ Children get an opportunity to be involved in a group project of gathering all the fishes, giving them the feeling of being part of the whole. Their ability to imagine is strengthened by adding the pretend element of catching the fish. When the fish are being gathered, point out or look for any that aren't caught ("Look, there's one! See any more?"). This enhances their focusing ability and also contributes to the feeling that they are helping to accomplish a larger task than just catching one.

♦ Children's eye-hand coordination and
   motor planning skills are also reinforced
   as they try to capture the ball with their
   strainers. Balls move differently in water
   than on land, and the children need to
   anticipate the movement to get the
   strainer in just the right position.

MODIFICATIONS

♦ If you have children who are still
   concrete learners and unable to
   play pretend, use materials, such
   as corks, that don't need to be
   "caught."

♦ To enhance communication and
   joint attention for more advanced children, ask them to point out
   to the less advanced children the "fish" that need to be caught ("Show
   Leanna where to find a fish").

♦ For children with dyspraxia (poor motor planning skills), use a
   hand-over-hand approach or gently guide their elbows to eliminate
   frustration.

Choo-Choo Train

*Making a choo-choo train is a fun group game anywhere, but it can be espe-
cially fun in the water.*

GOALS

Awareness of others
Shared attention

Holding on
Focusing
Pretending
Imitation
Vestibular, proprioceptive, and auditory stimulation

MATERIALS

Inner tubes
Pool
Life jackets

SETUP

An adult places each child in a tube. The tubes are then lined up, with each child holding on to the tube in front of her and the child in the very front holding on to an adult. Other adults should be either part of the train or supervising the children in the tubes.

DIRECTIONS

The adult in front acts as the "engineer" and begins to pull the rest of the train quickly through the water. The other adults are on the sides of the train helping the children to continually hold on to the tubes in front of them as well as helping the "engineer" move the train through the water.

Everyone makes trains sounds like "chugga chugga," "choo choo," or "whooo whooo."

VARIATIONS

1. The "engineer" can make quick turns or sudden stops and starts to increase the sensation of movements.

2. The "engineer" can alternate between fast and slow and stop and go, with another adult calling out the commands, such as "Go fast" or "Stop!" You might also use a visual to emphasize the command (for example, a stop sign or green and red colored materials, a bell, and so on).

WHAT IS BEING LEARNED

♦ Children are sharing the awareness of doing something with others. Their ability to hold on without being reminded or prompted can indicate the level of their awareness of being part of a group.

♦ When they make train sounds, they are engaging in the idea of pretending as well as imitating others.

♦ When the variations are used, the children's awareness of the meaning of the words "Stop," "Go," "Slow," and "Fast" is increased. The change in movement also keeps the children in the present.

♦ The sensation of moving through the resistance of water provides deep pressure, and the sudden changes in movement alert the nervous system.

MODIFICATIONS

♦ Children who cannot tolerate this level of unpredictable movement or closeness may need to stand back and watch. The adult can describe what the others are doing to keep the child involved in the experience.

♦ A child who is hypersensitive to touch and wants to avoid bumping into the others might prefer riding on the back of an adult when being part of the train.

Fill the Bucket

This is a popular game because the action is easy to understand: filling a cup with water and then pouring it into the bucket. The added spice is what happens after the bucket is full.

GOALS

Following directions
Auditory processing
Task completion
Sequencing
Shared attention

MATERIALS

One large bucket with a small hole on the side, near the bottom of the
  bucket
One small paper or plastic cup for each child
Water source

SETUP

Have children sit in a circle and give each one a cup. The bucket is in the
middle of the circle.

DIRECTIONS

Demonstrate filling the cup with water and pouring it into the bucket and
encourage everyone to do the same, all at the same time, while a song is
being sung.
  (Sung to the tune of "Skip to My Lou")

> Fill your cup and fill the bucket
> Fill your cup and fill the bucket,
> Fill your cup and fill the bucket,
> All the way to the top

When the bucket is full, point this out to the children, "Look, the bucket
is full, all the way to the top," or ask one of the children to look and decide
if the bucket is full.
  Then, lift the bucket over everyone's head and slowly turn in a circle
while the water runs out of the hole near the bottom of the bucket.

Encourage the children to put their empty cups under the stream of water to refill them.

Sing an appropriate song about water, such as:

> It's raining, it's pouring,
> The old man is snoring
> He went to bed and bonked his head
> And didn't get up in the morning.

Repeat the game at least three times so children can learn to follow directions and anticipate what will happen next.

VARIATIONS

1. If you don't want to make a hole in the bucket, gently pour the water on everyone's heads or body parts, including the adults!

2. Toss the water up in the air so that it falls down on everyone. Announce the move by saying "Waterfall!" so children anticipate the subsequent action.

WHAT IS BEING LEARNED

♦ Children are learning to follow the directions in the song. They will need to refill their cups many times and pour them into the bucket before the bucket is full.

♦ They are discovering the sequence to the game. First the cup is filled and emptied into the bucket, and then the bucket is filled and emptied.

♦ They are experiencing being part of a group project with a common goal of filling the bucket.

♦ In order to refill their cups from the stream of water coming out of the bucket hole, they need to notice how to place their cups in a strategic position.

♦ They are learning the words to a simple song and the appropriate time to sing.

Modifications

♦ At first, some children may need hand-over-hand help to fill and pour their cups.

♦ If children lose interest before the bucket is full, use a smaller bucket.

♦ For some children, the variations of pouring water on their heads or making a waterfall may be too much stimulation. For them, the water can be poured on their legs or other body parts, or not poured on them at all.

♦ To make it very clear when the bucket is full, draw a line in a contrasting color near the top. When the water hits the line, the bucket is full.

♦ If the players are more advanced, mark a line halfway or three-quarters of the way and modify the goal to only filling the bucket partway.

Floating on Your Back

Learning to relax is just as important as learning to move.

Goals

Relaxation

Tolerating change

Trust

Vestibular stimulation

MATERIALS

Pool
Life jackets

SETUP

None

DIRECTIONS

Tell the child she's going to float on her back and relax. Turn the child on her back and rest her head on your shoulder so it is out of the water.

Sing or hum a quiet tune to increase the feeling of calmness.

VARIATIONS

1. Place the child on her back on a boogie board or inflated raft.

2. Let the child float on his back independently with hips and head held afloat, but ears underwater.

WHAT IS BEING LEARNED

♦ The child is learning to trust that she will be safe with that adult and can not only learn to tolerate a new situation but also find that it is fun.

♦ She is also learning a way to relax her body.

MODIFICATIONS

♦ A child who finds it alarming to be on his back when held by an adult might be more comfortable on a raft.

Gecko Walking

Some animals, including geckos, walk alternating the left and right pairs of legs. In this imitation game, you can choose the name of the animal that fits your area. You can also easily transfer this game to land.

GOALS

Imitating an animal
Playing pretend
Following directions
Maneuvering the body through water
Alternating movement from one side of the body to the other
Strengthening the neck and back muscles
Proprioceptive stimulation

MATERIALS

Pool
Life jackets

SETUP

Have the child stand on all fours in shallow water or on a submerged ledge of a pool.

DIRECTIONS

Encourage the child to move forward in the water by alternating his left and right sides like a gecko or salamander.

Accompany the movement with a song, such as the following, sung to the tune of "Frère Jacques":

Gecko walking,
Gecko walking
To the end

To the end

You are gecko walking

You are gecko walking

To the end

To the end.

Make sure the child keeps her head above water at all times as she is moving forward.

VARIATIONS

1. Change the animal being imitated to a turtle. The movement would then be to advance forward with the arms and pull the legs after.

2. Have the children make believe they are porpoises and roll over in the water or jump up for pretend treats.

3. Transfer this skill and use this same idea on land, having children imitate a bear or kangaroo.

WHAT IS BEING LEARNED

♦ Movement through the water alerts and organizes the child's body and helps him pay attention to the moment.

♦ This is an opportunity to expand on the children's awareness of animals via movement.

♦ Children are also learning how to arrange their bodies so that their heads stay up and out of the water while they are moving through the water.

MODIFICATIONS

♦ For children who benefit from visual cues, have a picture of a gecko or lizard to show. Or, if doing variations, show pictures of a turtle crawling or a porpoise jumping. Other children might need to feel the desired movement by first experiencing it while riding on an adult's back. Have the adult lying prone and place the child on his back. The adult moves forward, exaggerating the side-to-side movement.

In and Out and Crash

Kids seem to relish crashing into each other. Many adults do too. Think bumper cars or football. This game has all the fun and none of the risk. Sensory seeking kids especially love to bump!

GOALS

Awareness of others

Proprioceptive stimulation

MATERIALS

One child-sized inner tube for each child

Pool

Life jackets

SETUP

Have all the children inside inner tubes and floating in a circle with adults standing behind them.

DIRECTIONS

The adults chant these words:

> In ... and ... out ... and
> In ... and ... out.
> In ... and out ...
> And in ... and ...
> Crash!

During the word "In," adults float the children into the center of the circle. On "Out," they float them back out to the edge of the circle. On the word "Crash," they bump the inner tubes into each other.

VARIATIONS

1. Vary the gentleness or the roughness of the crash depending on the children's reaction.

2. Vary the speed and distance on the in and out portion.

WHAT IS BEING LEARNED

♦ This sense of connecting to others in a fun but slightly jolting way that cannot be ignored is the essence of this game.

♦ Children are also experiencing the movements associated with the words "In" and "Out" and "Crash."

♦ After a few times of playing the game, they are learning to anticipate what comes next.

♦ They are also increasing their awareness of others by visually seeing them come closer, go farther away, and then physically bump into them.

MODIFICATIONS

♦ If one child has difficulty with the crashing aspect, let him still experience the in and out portion of the game, but hold his tube slightly away when others bump. Or encourage the child to say, "Stop" or put his hands up if he has had enough and wants to stop.

Into the Hole

This game is good for when the attention starts to get scattered and you want to bring it back. Place an inner tube for a target next to a child, hand him the ball to throw, and gather others up to have the next turn.

GOALS

Awareness of others
Turn taking

Shared attention
Handling attention
Eye-hand coordination
Proprioceptive stimulation
Modulation

MATERIALS

One inner tube
One ball—use a beach or larger ball if the inner tube is large
    and a small ball, such as a tennis ball, if the inner tube
    is smaller
Pool
Life jackets

SETUP

Have children make a circle in the pool, either being held or beside an
adult.

Have an inner tube floating in the center of the circle.

DIRECTIONS

Hand a ball to a child and ask her to toss it into the hole in the center of the
tube while the rest of the class chants her name:

"*Dora, Dora, Dora, Dora, Dora, Dora*" (the emphasis is on the last
    syllable).

When the ball is thrown into the tube, everyone cheers, "Yea!" the ball is
handed to the next child, and the sequence is repeated using the new child's
name.

If the child misses, say something like "Almost got it!" or "Try again" and
let the child have another turn until she is successful. If needed, the tube can
also be brought closer to the child, or the child can be physically helped, to
increase success.

V ARIATIONS

1. Place a floating object, such as a sponge, in the middle of the pool and have everyone take turns throwing hula hoops or other large rings around that object.

2. Place a floating toy in the middle of the pool that children try to dunk by hitting it with the ball.

W HAT I S B EING L EARNED

♦ Children are experiencing having the whole group's attention focused on them and having to perform. But as this moment only lasts a few seconds, it's easier to tolerate, and from this they can begin to expand their ability to handle attention for longer periods.

♦ Hearing the sound of one's own name said many times can add to a child's sense of being someone who is noticed and valued.

♦ Children are also learning that other children have names and having the opportunity to say those names.

♦ Children are also practicing their ability to coordinate the movement of their hands with the direction from their eyes and practicing modifying the amount of energy needed to put the ball through the hole.

M ODIFICATIONS

♦ For children who may need the game to be more challenging, have them stand further away from the target. Physically weaker or less coordinated children may need to be moved closer.

♦ Some children who may not understand the expectation will need physical prompting to help with throwing. Using a hand-over-hand technique encourages muscle memory by giving the child's body input on what the correct movement should feel like.

The Kids in the Water Go Splashy Clap

Here is a fun way to adapt the song "The Wheels on the Bus" to water.

GOALS

Playing with others
Imitating movement
Following directions
Auditory processing

MATERIALS

Kiddie pool, shallow end of a regular pool, or water table
Life jackets (if in a regular pool)

SETUP

Have the children sit in a circle in the pool or stand around the water table so that they can see each other.

DIRECTIONS

Sing this song as you do the actions described (sung to the tune of "The Wheels on the Bus"):
The kids in the water go splashy clap
(Clapping hands in a small amount of water so that they splash when clapped.)

Splashy clap
Splashy clap
The kids in the water go splashy clap
All day long.

Variations

1. Add a variety of movements and ask kids and other adults to come up with others. For example,

   The kids in the water:

   Go up and down

   Go in and out

   Go side to side

   Splash each other

   Kick their legs

   Flap their arms

   Wiggle their fingers

   Wag their heads

   Pat the water

   Swoosh the water, and so on.

2. Use a different song, such as "If You're Happy and You Know It" and make up different original ways to show your joy.

3. Do noises instead of movements. "The kids in the water say (cough, achoo, la la la, beadle beadle bum, and so forth)."

4. If you do the "in and out" movement variation, when children go into the center of the water, you can arrange for them to bump into each other. This will give them some physical feedback that there are others there.

What is Being Learned

♦ Children are learning to follow simple instructions. Because the instructions are given in song, it is easier for some children with ASD to hear them.

♦ It is also a way to give children the sense of enjoyment that can come from following the directions of others. When everyone is doing the same movements, it can help children feel connected to others and part of the group.

♦ So much is learned through imitation. Because this game encourages watching and copying, it sets the tone for other learning situations.

♦ While imitating, children need to figure out which muscles are being used to accomplish the task presented. What muscles are needed, for example, to swoosh the water? On an unconscious level, by watching and doing, they are learning to isolate just the right muscle group.

♦ When children are making movements underwater, they are experiencing working against the resistance of water, which can be very calming.

MODIFICATIONS

♦ Some children might need to be fully prompted physically to do the movements. If the child is sitting on the adult's lap, the adult is in a good position to help the child move from side to side or in and out, and to prompt the child to kick legs, and so on.

♦ After you give an instruction, wait a beat to see if the child is going to respond on his own. It might take a few seconds for him to process the direction. If there is no response, prompt or move the child's body parts accordingly.

♦ Some children will be uncomfortable if water gets splashed in their eyes. The idea is to make the activity enjoyable for this child as well as to stretch the number of things she can tolerate. At first, have this child clap with her hands above the water and just experience the splashing of others on her sides. As the game gets more familiar, experiment with more water in her clapping.

The Little Dutch Boy

It's empowering to know that you can make something happen, or not happen, just by using your thumb.

GOALS

Understanding of cause and effect
Working with others
Differentiating stop and go
Fine motor control

MATERIALS

Plastic water bottle

SETUP

Poke a small hole or holes in the lower sides of a plastic water bottle so that when the bottle is full, water pours out of the hole.

DIRECTIONS

Fill the bottle with water and show one or two children how the water pours out and how you can stop the water from flowing by putting a thumb over the hole.

Encourage the children to take turns stopping the water, or make two holes in the bottle so that each child can cover one of the holes with a finger.

VARIATIONS

1. Practice the concept of "stop and go" by having the child release the hole on a verbal cue.

2. Poke many holes in the bottle and let the water flow out. Hold the bottle above the child's head or other parts of her body so that she feels the flow. Sing a song, such as "It's Raining, It's Pouring" to accompany the game.

3. Make several well-placed holes so the child needs to use fingers *and* thumb to stop the water flow.

What Is Being Learned

♦ By stopping the water flow, children are learning that they have the ability to control an event.

♦ If they are doing the game with another, they experience working together to accomplish a goal.

Modifications

♦ To make the hole and where to place the finger more obvious, use permanent marker to draw a ring around the hole.

♦ Make the hole larger or smaller depending on the size of the child's hand.

Little Jumps, Big Jumps

Jumping the waves comes naturally to a child at the beach. In this game, we just make the height of the jump a purposeful and conscious decision.

Goals

Awareness of environment
Differences in energy output
Imitation of movement
Sharing activity
Anticipating action
Vestibular, visual, and proprioceptive stimulation

Materials

Ocean or large lake with little waves
Life jackets

Setup

Make sure that there are just little waves, gently lapping the shore.

DIRECTIONS

Standing at the water's edge or in shallow water, encourage the child or children to make little jumps over the small waves and bigger jumps over the bigger waves.

Help them anticipate the size of the jump by encouraging awareness of the wave that is coming next, "Here comes a big wave, get ready to jump high!" "Ahhhh, here is just a little wave, a ripple, let's just jump a little bit."

VARIATIONS

1. Have an adult and a child or two children face each other, hold both hands, and jump together.

2. Have a line of children and adults face the water, hold hands, and jump together.

WHAT IS BEING LEARNED

♦ Children are learning to anticipate and motor plan. They are noticing the differences in the size of the waves and are consciously using different levels of energy depending on the wave's size.

♦ They are noticing that they are imitating others and participating in a similar goal. When the action includes getting splashed or toppling over in the water's foam, they are also experiencing the fun of the sea.

MODIFICATIONS

♦ For children who are fearful at first, pick them up and hold them in your arms so they can concentrate on noticing the size of the waves and experience the sensation of your jumps.

♦ For children who are fearless or lack safety awareness, attach a small, soft rope to their life jackets so that they have the freedom to jump independently and you have the control over how far out they go!

London Bridge

This is an old game with a new twist. Instead of being made from arms, the bridge is made from foam "noodles" that lower to form the place where they "lock them up." This activity can also be done on land.

GOALS

Turn taking

Sequencing

Tolerating change

Anticipating predictable action

Vestibular stimulation

MATERIALS

Two foam "noodles"

Pool (optional)

Life jackets (if using the pool)

SETUP

Have two adults hold either end of the two noodles and form a bridge in the shallow end of the pool.

DIRECTIONS

Sing the traditional London Bridge song:

London Bridge is falling down

Falling down

Falling down

London Bridge is falling down

My fair children (instead of "My fair ladies")

Take the key and lock them up

Lock them up

Lock them up

Take the key and lock them up

My fair children

Children take turns going under the noodle bridge by moving in a circular pattern. First they go under the bridge, then around the adult holding one end, and finally back under the bridge. On the verse that starts with "Take the key," a child is caught between the two noodles and moved back and forth until the end of the verse.

The song is repeated until everyone has had a chance to get "locked up."

VARIATIONS

1. Catch more than one child at a time. Sometimes catch all the children at the same time!

2. Lower the noodles so that the children have to at least get their chins wet if not their whole heads while going under. Change the words slightly, singing:

    London Bridge is

    Way way down

    Way way down

    Way way down

    (and so on)

WHAT IS BEING LEARNED

♦ Children are learning to be part of a larger experience with others and taking turns.

♦ They are experiencing the sequencing of moving in a circular pattern and going under the bridge.

♦ They are learning to anticipate predictable action by seeing others getting caught and by experiencing it themselves.

♦ Children are also learning how to tolerate the direct attention of being caught and sung to.

♦ When caught, the child is held between the two noodles and swung from side to side, increasing vestibular awareness.

MODIFICATIONS

♦ Many children will need physical help from an adult to steer them in the right direction. As the game becomes increasingly familiar, reduce the amount of physical guidance. Start with holding the child and taking him under the bridge and progress to just giving standby assistance.

♦ Vary the amount of motion provided to the caught child. Increase it for children who need or want more stimulation. Decrease it for those who can't tolerate much.

Make a Pond

This game provides endless excuses to fill one's bucket with water as children try to make a pond that never fills up.

GOALS

Imitation of others
Group goal
Tactile stimulation
Proprioceptive and vestibular stimulation
Sequencing

MATERIALS

Sandy beach
Small buckets
Life jackets
Optional: beach shovels

SETUP

Children and adults sit around a central flat spot in the sand near the water.

DIRECTIONS

Have everyone work together to dig a large hole in the sand using shovels or just hands.

Once the hole is dug, give the children buckets to fill up with ocean or lake water to dump into the hole. Give them the image that they are filling up the hole to make a pond or pool.

VARIATIONS

1. Place a bucket in the hole and make the surrounding sand flush with the top of the bucket. Because water quickly leaks through the sand, the filled bucket makes a more clear-cut ending to the goal.

2. Have a child sit in the hole and pour the water around and on the child in the "pond."

WHAT IS BEING LEARNED

♦ This game encourages working toward a joint goal so that children experience being part of a group process.

♦ Carrying the water to dump in the hole requires the awareness of sequences. First the child must scoop the water from the ocean, then walk over to the hole, then dump the water.

♦ Carrying the bucket increases muscle strength and alerts the proprioceptive system with heavy work, which can also be calming.

♦ Walking on the uneven surfaces of the sand is challenging and increases children's sense of balance by stimulating their vestibular systems.

MODIFICATIONS

♦ Children who have difficulty with sequencing and staying focused will need a lot of physical prompts to follow the directions along with the verbal cues, "Now we go get the water," "Now we are scooping up the ocean water," and so on. They may need an adult or more experienced child to stay with them to keep them on task.

Monkey Walking

"Monkey walking" helps a child begin to be independent in the water by allowing him to hold on to the pool's rim while moving.

GOALS

Synchronized movement with others
Motor planning through body awareness
Establishing independence in the pool
Increasing confidence and autonomy

MATERIALS

Pool
Life jackets

SETUP

Have children hold on to the side of the pool with their feet either hanging down or on the pool wall.

An adult should be beside each child or, if needed, behind the child and also holding on to the sides of the pool.

DIRECTIONS

Have children move sideways along the edge of the pool by alternating the positioning of the hands and feet. Either go along the entire length of the pool this way, or from one designated spot to another.

Chant these words as the children move along:

Monkey walking

Monkey walk

Monkey walking

Monkey walk

Monkey walking

Monkey walk

All the way to the end

When you get to the end, reverse direction and return to the starting point.

VARIATIONS

1. This can be done in shallow water so that children can walk sideways against the resistance of water.

2. This can be done just using the arms to move sideways and letting the feet dangle.

3. Two children or an adult and a child can do this together when one person is behind the other.

WHAT IS BEING LEARNED

♦ Children feel more in control while in a pool knowing that they have the ability to move along the edge.

♦ They are learning to coordinate the movements of their arms or their legs and arms together to accomplish a goal.

♦ Because they are moving in concert with one another, their awareness of being part of a group is enhanced. When they reverse directions, they need to move together to avoid collisions.

MODIFICATIONS

♦ Almost all children seem to learn this movement fairly easily because it includes the security of holding on to the side of the pool.

♦ Some children might have difficulty with the correct movement of hands and would benefit from having an adult behind them. The adult places his hands on the child's and moves the child's hands in unison with his own.

One, Two, Three–Change

Getting comfortable with a variety of people is a challenge for many of us, and especially for kids with ASD. Here's a lighthearted way to experiment with changes.

GOALS

Dealing with change
Greeting strangers

MATERIALS

One inner tube per child
Pool
Life jackets

SETUP

Put each child in an inner tube and have the adults form an open circle in the pool with a child in front of them. The water should be shallow enough so that the adults can stand.

DIRECTIONS

Adults begin to chant, "One, two, three—change", and on the word "Change," everyone gently pushes their child's inner tube to their left and to the next person in the circle. The waiting adult encourages the child to paddle toward him and greets her by name. Again, the "One, two, three—change" call is said and the children continue on to the next person in the circle until back with the person they started with. In this step-by-step way, each child has contact with each adult.

According to the needs of the group, adjust the pace of the game and how quickly the changes are made. Start the game slowly and, as children get used to what is happening, slightly speed it up.

As the game gets more familiar, add rowdier variations so that the novelty of the added movements enhances the children's alertness.

In the beginning, do at least one round with everyone having a chance to be with everyone else. Later, continue the game for three or four rounds.

VARIATIONS

1. Add a new greeting. When the child arrives at the next adult, have them exchange a high five or a handshake.

2. Add a twirling movement. When the child arrives at the next adult, his inner tube is twirled by rotating it around in a circle or, holding hands, adult and child twirl in a circle together.

3. Add lifts. The child is picked up, in the inner tube, and thrown lightly in the air, before being placed back in the water.

WHAT IS BEING LEARNED

♦ This game addresses the difficulty that some children have with being with new people and with making changes. In this game, change happens quickly but consistently. There is the letting go of the familiar and the pleasant sensation of going through water, leading to a brief moment of relating to someone new.

♦ The continual pleasure of being surrounded by water in a friendly setting makes this usually troublesome adjustment easier to handle. It helps children to see that meeting a new person can be a safe and pleasant experience.

MODIFICATIONS

◆ For the child who finds change too frightening at this point, have her make the changes in the arms of a familiar adult. The adult and the child together go from adult to adult. Later, when the other adults become more familiar and the game predictable, have the child do it on her own.

◆ Or, at first, keep the circle small so that the child who is uncomfortable with leaving his familiar adult returns quickly to that person.

◆ As the game becomes more familiar and predictable, keep enlarging the circle so the children are able to travel longer distances between adults before returning to the familiar adult.

◆ Purposely make eye contact with the children during the greeting part to give those for whom eye contact may be difficult a chance to try it briefly in an activity in which there are no prolonged expectations.

◆ Some children who crave vestibular and proprioceptive input love to get thrown rather than floated from person to person. These are the children who are already comfortable with going under the water and know how to close their mouths to keep the water out.

◆ Know which children have potential respiratory problems so that care is taken not to get water in their mouths.

Parallel Swim

Having someone call to children encouragingly can help them learn a new skill, in this case, swimming on their own.

GOALS

Following directions

Anticipating a goal

Motor planning (conscious use of muscles to achieve a goal)

Awareness of others

MATERIALS

Pool

Inner tube

Life jackets

SETUP

Have two adults stand a short distance apart in the pool with one adult holding the child in an inner tube or life jacket facing the other adult.

DIRECTIONS

Give the instruction, "Swim to Jerry," or whatever name identifies the other adult. Give as much or as little help as needed to propel the child in the right direction.

Add verbal cues, such as "Kick your legs" or "Use your arms," and give some physical prompts, when appropriate.

When the child reaches the goal of arriving at the other person, make a big deal out of saying, "You did it!"

Have the child swim back and forth between the adults for a while.

VARIATIONS

1. Two children can play this at the same time, each one going to the other adult.

2. In subsequent sessions, enlarge the distance between the adults.

WHAT IS BEING LEARNED

♦ The child is having the experience of achieving a goal. If the child was initially fearful about being in the water independently, the ability to be on her own, however briefly, will increase her sense of autonomy.

♦ She is learning to coordinate the movements of her upper and lower halves to propel herself forward. This ability to move the halves of the body separately but in concert is needed for other motor activities, such as jumping and running.

♦ The social awareness of pleasing others and the pleasure of receiving praise is also present.

♦ The pressure of moving through the water both alerts and calms the child.

MODIFICATIONS

♦ Some children are fearful of not being held while in the water. Provide enough tactile pressure to calm the child so that she feels safe, or make the distance between adults very small. With time, decrease touch and replace it with encouraging words, such as "You're OK," "You're doing it," or "I'm right here."

Ping-Pong Play

Ping-Pong balls are always fun to play with. They are just the right size for little hands, they move slowly enough in the water to hit easily, and they move erratically enough to add a challenge.

GOALS

Focusing
Eye-hand coordination
Proprioceptive feedback

MATERIALS

Ping-Pong paddle for each child
One Ping-Pong ball with a happy face painted on it

Kiddie pool, shallow end of a regular pool, or water table

Life jackets

SETUP

Have the children and adults sit in a small pool or stand in a circle in shallow water.

DIRECTIONS

Give each player a Ping-Pong paddle and have them push the Ping-Pong ball in the water from player to player. All the children are encouraged to watch the ball and see where it goes.

When the ball comes into a child's space, he pushes it away with his paddle.

VARIATIONS

1. Use hands rather than paddles to bat the balls.

2. Use a larger ball, such as a tennis ball, or an even larger ball, such as a beach ball, to make the game even more obvious.

WHAT IS BEING LEARNED

♦ Being able to focus on an object without getting distracted is a necessary skill for learning, and one that can be difficult for children. This game gives them an opportunity to try and stay aware of what is happening, because at any moment they will get the chance to bat at the ball.

♦ Because moving a paddle through the resistance of water is "heavy work," they are getting the feedback from their joints and nerves that can help alert and calm them.

♦ They are also getting an opportunity to practice eye-hand coordination.

MODIFICATIONS

♦ If some kids have trouble understanding the game, start with only two players so that the idea of the game is understood and each child gets many turns. Once the game is familiar, do it with more children in a circle formation.

- Some children may need the adult to help them hit the ball at the right moment.
- Help some children to stay attentive to the action by pointing out who hit the ball, "Look, Sarah hit the ball to Kyle."

Ready? Set. Jump!

Jumping on cue takes preparation, waiting, anticipating, and then action. But kids just know that jumping is fun!

GOALS

Responding to verbal cues
Timing
Overcoming fear
Motor planning
Tolerating change
Proprioceptive, vestibular, and auditory stimulation

MATERIALS

Pool
Life jackets

SETUP

Have the child stand by the edge of the pool while an adult waits in the water in front of him. If the pool has an inside ledge, begin this activity at this lower level.

DIRECTIONS

The adult should hold her arms out to the child and say, "Ready . . . set . . . jump!" encouraging the child to jump on the final word.

If the child is reluctant to jump, the adult should initially hold her under her armpits and lift her into the air before gently placing her in the water.

At the next level of competence, the adult should place her hands on the child's trunk to guide her when to jump.

At the next level, the child should be able to propel herself and the adult should catch her and control how deeply she goes into the water.

At the final level, the child can jump in herself and go under the water before coming up.

V A R I A T I O N S

1. Two children hold hands and jump together or just jump at the same time.

2. While saying, "One, two, three, jump," have the children imitate holding up the right amount of fingers to show each number before jumping.

W H A T I S B E I N G L E A R N E D

♦ Children are learning to overcome the fear of transitions by experiencing the sudden changing from one medium to another (air into water).

♦ They are learning to listen to cues to jump with the correct timing. Timing takes an internal awareness of what their bodies are doing as they motorically plan to bend before pushing off at the word "Jump."

♦ They are practicing their ability to trust others as they launch themselves into waiting arms or drop into the water, knowing that they will come up and be OK.

M O D I F I C A T I O N S

♦ Some children will step off into the water rather than jumping. Show them how to bend their knees first and then push off.

♦ Some children get distracted or anxious and run off in another direction. For those children, use two adults for this activity. Have one adult stand behind the child, gently squeezing her shoulders and arms or compressing the shoulder joints to help calm her. The adult in the water lifts or guides the child into the pool after saying the cue words.

♦ Children who are hyporesponsive to movement will need the additional exhilarating and alerting sensation of being lifted high in the air before being splashed in the water. You're likely to find that they want this game repeated many times!

Riding the Horse Noodles

Riding a "noodle" is like riding a horse, but much easier.

GOALS

Playing pretend
Awareness of others
Balance
Muscle isolation
Vestibular stimulation

MATERIALS

Two foam "noodles"
Pool
Life jackets

SETUP

Have an adult show the child how to put the noodle between his legs so that he is sitting in the middle of the noodle and holding on to the top half with both hands. When the child is on the noodle, the adult also gets on the noodle.

DIRECTIONS

The adult should tell the child that they are pretending the noodles are horses and they are going to make them go using your legs. Show her by example or with physical prompts how to paddle her feet so that she moves forward in the water.

Pretend to be racing each other with appropriate vocals, such as "Giddyap horsey" and "Yippee!"

VARIATIONS

1. Have several children do it together and have a race.

2. Have two children ride one noodle horse together.

WHAT IS BEING LEARNED

♦ Children are developing imagination by pretending the noodle is a horse.

♦ They are enhancing their sense of balance by sitting upright on the noodle horse.

♦ They are also learning how to isolate and move their lower extremities to accomplish the goal of moving forward in the water.

MODIFICATIONS

♦ For the child who is unable to accomplish this by himself due to poor trunk balance or fearfulness, place him on the same noodle as the adult, sitting in front. Or have a child with more advanced skill ride with the child who is less skilled.

Ring-Around-a-Rosy

Most people know this game. It's a wonderful way for a group of kids to play in a circle together. The fun of doing it in the water is the change in the ending. Instead of falling down, kids jump into the water.

GOALS

Timing
Listening
Shared attention
Motor planning (praxia)
Vestibular stimulation
Auditory stimulation

MATERIALS

Kiddie pool

SETUP

Alternate children and adults in a circle around the kiddie pool.

DIRECTIONS

Sing the traditional "Ring-Around-a-Rosy" tune with a slight variation in the words, as you walk in a circle around the pool.

> Ring around a rosy
> A pocket full of posies
> Bend your knees
> And . . .
> Jump in!

When the phrase "Bend your knees" is sung, adults model by bending their knees as in preparation for a jump. On the words "And jump in," the adults on either side of a child help her jump into the pool.

VARIATIONS

1. Once children have learned the game very well, experiment with having the children form their own circle without help from the adults.

2. While going around in the circle, instead of just walking, lift legs as if marching.

3. Try different endings, such as "All kick the water," "All jump up," or "All run into the middle." The variety encourages following directions and imitating movements and brings in novelty.

WHAT IS BEING LEARNED

♦ Children are learning to match their movements with words.

♦ They are learning to anticipate what is coming next.

♦ They are learning the words to a song and experiencing singing it with others.

MODIFICATIONS

♦ Some children have difficulty with timing, motor planning, or following verbal cues. They might jump too soon or too late. Hold the word "And" for a beat or two and then really emphasize the words "Jump in!!!" to help them see the connection. Or use a visual cue, such as throwing a ball into the pool on the word "Jump" or waving a red bandanna.

♦ Fade the visual cues as they learn to attend to the verbal ones.

♦ When introducing the game, start slowly so that children have time to notice and imitate the "Bend your knees" portion. Bending their knees first helps children who are new to jumping to get into correct positioning.

Save Your Life

It can be fun to pretend your life is in danger and that you are able to save yourself. It's also good practice to know you could save yourself if you needed to.

GOALS

Sense of independence
Awareness of safety
Pretending

MATERIALS

Pool

Life jackets

SETUP

An adult places the child in the water a short distance from the edge of the pool. This game is for the child who is already comfortable in the water and has the cognition to understand the game.

DIRECTIONS

An adult asks a child, "Can you swim to the edge of the pool by yourself? Do you want to try now?" If the answer is yes for both questions, say, "Are you ready? When I count to three, I'm going to let go and you are going to swim by yourself. Ready—one, two, three—save your life!"

When the child reaches the edge, give lots of praise, "You did it! You did it!" Some little ones enjoy being physically rewarded by being tossed up in the air and caught, along with the verbal praise.

VARIATIONS

1. Over time, keep increasing the distance that the child swims.

2. Have two or more children do the game at the same time. Or have one child who would be a role model for the other go first.

WHAT IS BEING LEARNED

♦ Children are learning the correct direction to go for safety. If, at another time, they find themselves alone, they already will have had practice in saving themselves and will be less likely to panic.

♦ They are learning that they can be independent in the pool when wearing a life jacket and they are also developing a sense of competence in their abilities.

♦ They are also getting an opportunity to practice pretending to be in danger and overcoming it.

MODIFICATIONS

♦ This activity is for children who have already shown that they have a sense of humor and playfulness and not for the child who is more concrete in her thinking and would take the game seriously. To develop the same skills in these children, do the same activity, but instead of telling them to save themselves, just encourage them to "Swim to the edge."

Shark Attack

Pretending to be afraid of some kind of monster is always fun. Change the name, if you want, to the creature of your choice.

GOALS

Joint attention
Sequencing
Pretending
Overcoming fear
Vestibular stimulation

MATERIALS

Pool
Life jackets
Optional: a pretend shark fin hat (or other kind of hat) to help bridge
    the difference between the concrete and pretend

SETUP

One adult should hold a child in the pool. Another pretends to be a shark by holding up a flat palm at his forehead or wearing a shark hat.

DIRECTIONS

Have the shark say to child, "I'm going to get you. You'd better run." The adult holding the child should pretend to be afraid and start running in the water carrying the child away from the shark. They keep running, looking back at the shark, until the shark catches them and tickles the child or pretends to eat them.

Next, switch roles so that the adult and child pretend to be the shark and the former shark turns and runs away.

It's more fun and clearer to the children if the person running away exaggerates his fear by throwing his arms in the air and saying, "Help! Help!"

VARIATIONS

1. Keep prolonging the length of the chase and increase the amount of time the child is in the present moment.

2. Involve other people in the game. They can be hiding behind someone else, asking for help, running away, or helping the shark.

WHAT IS BEING LEARNED

♦ Like an amusement park ride that seems dangerous but really isn't, this shark attack gives children an opportunity to overcome fear. It gives them a moment to allow unpredictability and loss of control, which turns out to be OK and even fun.

♦ Being afraid also stimulates awareness of the present moment by increasing the adrenaline. Yet the children can feel that excitement and still know they are safe in their adult's arms.

♦ Because no one runs very fast in the water, it all takes place in a kind of slow motion that gives the child a chance to understand what is happening and the rules of the game: to chase and be chased.

♦ Children also are learning the sequence of being the chaser and the one who is chased.

MODIFICATIONS

♦ If a child is genuinely afraid, start small so that the children learn quickly that getting attacked means getting tickled or hugged or whatever action each particular child enjoys. Children who are hyporesponsive to vestibular input may prefer something more energetic than tickling, such as roughhousing. For the child who has tactile hypersensitivities, tickling might be replaced with a gentle squeeze.

◆ For children who have difficulty with pretending, a photo of a shark could be used to help the child understand what he is supposed to be. Later, phase out the props of the hat and the photo.

◆ If sharks are too scary, use a milder creature like a "tickle monster." The tickle monster can be in the center of a circle of kids and pretend to go after them one by one Kids can take turns being the tickle monster.

The Sponge Pass

Waiting for one's turn can be hard for anyone, even for adults in a supermarket line. In this game, kids find that it's worth waiting for something fun.

GOALS

Turn taking
Shared attention
Understanding of cause and effect
Following directions
Rhythm practice
Modulation
Tactile stimulation

MATERIALS

Large sponge
Kiddie pool or water table

SETUP

Have children sit in a circle in the water or stand around the water table. They should have already played a few group games everyone could play at once, such as Fill the Bucket. And if they have already had a chance to be active, they will be better able to handle waiting for a turn.

DIRECTIONS

First demonstrate the actions to the words below. Chant the words or add a tune to the words. For example, this song is sung to the tune of "Skip to My Lou":

> Dip the sponge and squeeze it hard
>
> Dip the sponge and squeeze it hard
>
> Dip the sponge and squeeze it hard
>
> Pass it to your friend

Exaggerate the action so the movement is very obvious to the children. Dip the sponge deeply into the water on the word "Dip" and, when squeezing the sponge on the word "Squeeze," make a grunting face as your fingers wring the sponge.

Each child has the whole length of the lyric to play with getting the sponge soaking wet and squeezing it before they have to pass it to the next person. Children are encouraged to make eye contact when passing and put their hands out when receiving.

The plan is that children will do the movements to match the words of the song, but you may have to slow the words to match the child's movements. "Dip the sponge annnnnnnnnnnnnnnnnnd squeeze it tight."

While the sponge is making its way around the circle, the adults can encourage shared attention by pointing out where the sponge is now. "Justin has the sponge and soon he will give it to Jimmy and soon it will be your turn."

VARIATIONS

1. Use different objects on different days to expand the experience. For example, use watering cans, squirt guns, turkey basters, or any plastic instrument

that can be filled with water and emptied. Other kinds of objects that are unusual to use, such as rotary mixers and funnels, capture children's attention and are worth waiting for. Change the words to the song to match the action: for example, when using a turkey baster, sing:

Fill the tube, then squeeze it out

Squeeze it out

Squeeze it out

Fill the tube, then squeeze it out

Pass it to your friend

WHAT IS BEING LEARNED

◆ Children are learning to watch when it is someone else's turn and to wait for their own turns. The rhythm of the song lets them know how long each turn will take and gives them hope that their turn is coming soon.

◆ They are getting a chance to explore items and learn how to make them work. Objects that are novel to children increase the interest level.

◆ They are having the opportunity to hear directions and imitate matching their movements to the words, as well as to grade their movements to be the appropriate intensity.

MODIFICATIONS

◆ It can take a while for some children to be agreeable to the "Pass it to your friend" part, and they may need reassurance that they will get another turn.

◆ If they have a hard time waiting, use two similar objects, such as two sponges of different colors, and have them both going around the circle in different directions so kids don't have to wait as long for their turns.

♦ Children can also play the "my turn, your turn" game with an adult beforehand. In these practice sessions, the adult takes a very short turn before giving the item back to the child.

The Squirting Game

There is something about snowball fights and squirting games that always raises the level of excitement.

GOALS

Joint attention
Experiencing back-and-forth play
Understanding of cause and effect
Enlarging tactile tolerance
Tactile and visual stimulation

MATERIALS

Squirt toys (instead of or in addition to guns you can buy little creatures, such as frogs and fishes, that squirt)

SETUP

Fill the squirt toys with water and put them in a bag or bucket.

DIRECTIONS

Bring out a bag of squirt toys and say, "Who wants a toy?" Children need to respond at whatever level they can, from saying, "Me, please" to making a palms-up hand gesture or sound.

Begin squirting while saying, "I'm going to squirt you" in a fun voice. Start by squirting the children who are most likely to respond. When they squirt back, exaggerate your response by falling over or making a grand "I'm hit" gesture. It's delightful to see children get the humor of it and laugh heartily at an adult's response.

Keep the back-and-forth play going for as long as the interest lasts. To announce the end of the game, bring out the bag the toys were in and sing a familiar "Clean Up" song.

VARIATIONS

1. Use a cup instead of a squirt toy and pour water on each other's heads or other body parts.

2. When you're in a pool, splash each other.

WHAT IS BEING LEARNED

♦ Children are learning the give-and-take of playing. They are learning how to play pretend and read another's response through their gestures and body language. Mostly they are seeing that this kind of give-and-take can be silly and satisfying fun.

MODIFICATIONS

♦ For the concrete thinker who finds this game too threatening or the child who finds the action overstimulating, have her just watch while sitting snugly on your lap as you describe the action. "Jimmy is squirting Jerry, and Jerry is laughing and pretending to fall over."

♦ If you use the variation of pouring water and the child doesn't like it, try pouring water on a part of the body that is less sensitive, such as the legs or feet, to help desensitize her reaction. Or encourage her to pour water on you or have another adult help her to do that, and you exaggerate being surprised, "What—you poured water on me!"

♦ If a child does not respond, try to elicit a response by being direct. "I'm going to squirt your arm. Are you ready? Tell me yes or no. Yes? OK. One, two, three—squirt!"

Tug the Tube

If you've known the fun of playing Tug-of-War with a rope, you'll see why kids like Tug the Tube.

GOALS

Shared attention
Focusing
Muscle strengthening
Pretend play
Proprioceptive stimulation

MATERIALS

Pool
Life jackets
Child-sized inner tube

SETUP

Adults and children should sit in a circle in very shallow water. Each child is sitting beside an adult or on an adult's lap. An inner tube is placed in the center of the circle.

DIRECTIONS

The children are encouraged to hold on to the tube. A hand-over-hand method is used, if needed, to encourage children to hold on.

Half the group pulls the tube toward themselves while the other half pulls the tube in the opposite direction. A playful "tug-of-war" ensues. Adults model such words as "It's ours!" and "No, it's ours!"

The game continues until one side pulls the inner tube away from the others.

Grown-ups on the losing side can exaggerate their falling forward. The winning team makes triumphant sounds.

V A R I A T I O N S

1. Do the game in deeper water with the adults standing and holding their children or with their children in other inner tubes of their own.

2. Make this a back-and-forth game between only two children.

W H A T   I S   B E I N G   L E A R N E D

♦ Proprioceptive input can have a powerful calming and organizing effect on the nervous system. Pulling stimulates the proprioceptive system, giving the nervous system more feedback. For children with autism and SPD, this feedback alerts the child that there is something going on and encourages her to check out what is happening externally, increasing her awareness of others. Because the atmosphere is playful, children get a chance to practice pretending to be in a mock battle.

♦ Children also have the opportunity to develop the sense that they are part of a larger team and are working together to accomplish a goal.

♦ For the child who has physical weakness or undeveloped musculature, this activity of pulling against resistance increases muscle strength.

♦ For the hyperactive child who craves more movement, this tugging allows this need yet also contains it to a focused area. If playing in deep water, children are free to move their legs against the resistance of water, which also satisfies their need for more movement, but in an appropriate way.

M O D I F I C A T I O N S

♦ Modify the aggressiveness of the tugging and the noise level for children with low tolerance for sound and movement. Try increasing children's tolerance by holding them securely during the game to increase their sense of safety.

Wa-Wa-Wa-Water!

Sometimes the anticipation of a fun experience is just as exciting as the experience itself.

GOALS

Anticipation
Imitation
Sequencing
Working in concert with others
Vestibular and proprioceptive stimulation

MATERIALS

Kiddie pool, shallow end of a regular pool, or water table
Life jackets

SETUP

Have the children sit in a circle in shallow water or stand around the water table so that they can see each other and the leader.

DIRECTIONS

Say the word:
"Wa
Wa
Wa
Wa—ter"

As you say the word, swirl the water around enticingly for the "Wa Wa's," with palms up, and then lift up handfuls of water in the palms of your hands and let it trickle out on the final "Wa—ter."

Encourage children to copy the action.

VARIATIONS

1. Instead of lifting up water on the last word, pat the water to make it splash. How vigorously you pat the water depends on the mood and needs of the children.

2. Use a similar anticipatory sound when doing other movements, such as "K-K-K-Kick!"

WHAT IS BEING LEARNED

♦ Children are learning to anticipate a fun experience. They are experiencing rhythm and timing by learning how long they make the beginning sound before they get to splash the water. They are being part of a group doing the same thing, so they are getting to see the fun in togetherness.

♦ The predictability of the activity is also satisfying and helps them to expand their repertoire of familiar experiences.

MODIFICATIONS

♦ It can be fun for children to splash the water or it can be irritating. If a child does not like the splashing element, modify the game by using just the fingers for swirling. Or play a different variation, such as the "K-K-K Kick" idea.

♦ Some children may need verbal or physical prompts to imitate the movements.

Index of Games by Sensory System or Skill Stimulated

Although each game encourages many aspects of development, the games below are divided according to the system or skill most stimulated.

Proprioceptive

A Kid Sandwich
Are You My Mummy?
Blanket Ride
Going Through the Tunnel of Legs
Make a Pond
Name Game
Ping-Pong Play

Rolling Children
Sausage Roll
Scarf Toss
Sink the Boat
Styrofoam Hammering
Tug-of-War
Tug the Tube

Visual

Bingo Game
Bubble Blowing
Catch a Fish
Cereal Box Puzzles
Cereal Necklace
Drawing Faces
Feather Blowing
"I'm Here!"
Penny Flick
Point to the Cup
Scarf Toss
Secret Message
Sink the Boat
Stack the Cans
Target Games
The Little Dutch Boy
Toothpick Treats
What's in the Sock?
Who Is This?
Wiggling Snake
Yes-No Game

Vestibular

Are You My Mummy?
Balloon Baseball
Blanket Ride
Boat Ride
Boogie Board Ride
Feather Blowing
Gecko Walking
Hammock Swing
Jump to Colors
Leap the Shoes
Make a Pond
Monkey Walking
Obstacle Course
Ready? Set. Jump!
Riding the Horse Noodles
Sausage Roll
Tug-of-War
We Are Rocking
Wiggling Snake

Tactile

Are You My Mummy?
Bury the Body
Dump and Fill

Eyedropper Squirts
Lost in Rice
Pudding Party
Sausage Roll
Styrofoam Hammering
The Little Dutch Boy
Wa-Wa-Wa-Water!
What's in the Sock?

Auditory

Fill the Bucket
"I'm Here!"
Listening Game
Little Jumps, Big Jumps
Ring-Around-a-Rosy
Sound Makers
Who's in the Box?
Yes-No Game

Motoric

Into the Hole
Balloon Baseball
Bingo Game
Catch a Fish
Cereal Necklace

Colored Slots
Dump and Fill
Eyedropper Squirts
Jump to Colors
Little Jumps, Big Jumps
Parallel Swim
Penny Flick
Ping-Pong Play
Races
Ready? Set. Jump!
Save Your Life
Scarf Toss
Sink the Boat
Stack the Cans
Stop and Go
Styrofoam Hammering
Target Games
Throw the Balls into the Box
Throwing Through the Tube
Toothpick Treats
Walk with Rhythm
Wiggling Snake

Oral Motor and Communication

Blow Bubbles and Hum
Bubble Blowing
Feather Blowing
"I'm Here!"
Point to the Cup

RurRurRurRurRUN!
Straw Sucking
Wa-Wa-Wa-Water
Who's in the Box?
Yes-No Game

Social

A Kid Sandwich
Blanket Ride
Box Ride
Bury the Body
Choo-Choo Train
Colored Slots
Dump and Fill
In and Out and Crash
Name Game
One, Two, Three—Change
Parallel Swim
Penny Flick
Ring-Around-a-Rosy
Rolling Children
Sausage Roll
Shark Attack
The Squirting Game
Stack the Cans
The Kids in the Water Go Splashy Clap
Tug-of-War
Who's in the Box?

Turn Taking

Balloon Baseball
Box Ride
Colored Slots
Dump and Fill
London Bridge
Ping-Pong Play
Smelling Game
The Sponge Pass

Calming

Are You My Mummy?
Boat Ride
Box Ride
Cereal Necklace
Feather Blowing
Hammock Swing
Massaging
Pudding Party
Sausage Roll

APPENDIX II

Additional Resources

Information and Organizations

Alert Program (Mary Sue William and Sherry Shellenberger):
www.alertprogram.com

AOTA Special Interest Sensory Integration and Early Intervention:
www.aota.org; www.aota.org/search.aspx?SearchPhrase=sensory1
integration

Autism and Asperger's Digest: www.autismdigest.com/

Autism Network for Dietary Intervention (ANDI): www.autismndi.com

Autism Society of America: www.autism-society.org/site/PageServer

Carol Kranowitz: www.out-of-sync-child.com/

DAN! (Defeat Autism Now): www.defeatautismnow.com

Daniel Hawthorne: www.tbns.net/danielrh/

Developmental Delay Resources: www.devdelay.org/

Feingold Diet: www.feingold.org

Greenspan, Stanley DIR*/Floortime: Developmental, Individual differences and Relationship components: www.floortime.org

Integrations Catalog: www.integrationscatalog.com

Jene Aviram's Natural Learning Concepts (autism and special needs tools): www.nlconcepts.com

Lucy Jane Miller's Sensory Processing Disorder Foundation: www.SPDFoundation.net

Picture Exchange Communication (PECS): www.spectronicsinoz.com

Pivotal Response Training: www.dbpeds.org/articles/detail.cfm?TextID=229

Play Project-Training Program: www.playproject.org

Pocket Full of Therapy (pediatric and school - based products): www.pfot.com

Right Start (eco - friendly equipment for young children): www.rightstart.com

Sensory Resources: www.SensoryResources.com

SPD Canada Foundation: www.spdcanada.org

Star Program: www.starprogram.org/

SticKids (software and activities for sensory processing differences) www.SticKids.com

TACA (Talk About Curing Autism): www.talkaboutcuringautism.org/index.htm

The Gray Center—Carol Gray's Social Stories Web Site: www.thegraycenter.com

Vision Therapy: www.vision-therapy.com

Zosia Zaks: www.autismability.com

Therapy and Play Ideas

Abilitation Integration (therapy equipment): www.abilitation.com

Barbara Sher's games: www.gameslady.com

Carol Kranowitz's Out-of-Sync Child: www.out-of-sync-child.com

Henry OT Services and Diana Henry: www.ateachabout.com

OT Exchange: www.otexchange.com

Right Brain Learning: www.DianneCraft.com

Therapy Bookshop (Australia; books on autism):
    www.therapybookshop.com

Therapy Products: www.theraproducts.com

Therapy Shoppe (for fun fine motor tools and more):
    www.therapyshoppe.com

Parent Listservs (Parent Support)

Ida Zelaya's Sensory Street: www.sensorystreet.com

Parent Forum: www.parent-forum.com

Tips for parents of children with SPD: www.spdconnection
    .com/parenttips.htm

The Author - - - - - - - - - - - - - - - - - -

Barbara Sher is a mother, grandmother, and an occupational therapist who has worked for over thirty-five years with children who have special needs. Her unique style is to go into the classrooms and play a fun, active, learning game with all the children, including "her" special child, so that everyone can enjoy playing and learning together. She also uses small groups, such as "Social Club" and "aquatherapy," for therapeutic intervention.

She has given workshops on playing games and making homemade educational toys in many countries, including Cambodia, Honduras, Hong Kong, and New Zealand. Her books have been translated into a large variety of languages, including Chinese, Swedish, Hebrew, Arabic, and Estonian. Her games reach across cultures and touch the spirit of all children.

She spends the school year working in the Northern Mariana Islands and the summers in Northern California, near her daughters and grandchildren.

She is the author of *Attention Games: 101 Fun Easy Games That Help Kids Learn to Focus* (Wiley); *Smart Play: 101 Fun Easy Games That Enhance Intelligence* (Wiley); *Self-Esteem Games: 300 Fun Activities That Make Children Feel Good About Themselves* (Wiley); *Spirit Games: 300 Fun Activities That Bring Children Comfort and Joy* (Wiley); *Extraordinary Play with Ordinary Things: Motor Games with Everyday Stuff* (Bright Baby Books); *Playful Moments: Spontaneous Games to Play with Your Young* (Bright Baby Books); and *Homegrown Babies: Gentle Ways of Enriching Babies Development* (Bright Baby Books).

For more details, see www.gameslady.com

Bibliography - - - - - - - - - - - - - -

Angermeir, Patricia, Joan Krzyzanowski, and Kristina Moiir. *Learning in Motion.* Las Vegas, NV: Sensory Resources, 1998.

Aquilla, Paula, Ellen Yack, and Shirley Sutton, OT. *Building Bridges Through Sensory Integration.* 2nd ed. Las Vegas, NV: Sensory Resources, 2009.

Armstrong, Thomas. *The Myth of the ADD Child.* New York: Plume, 1997.

Ayres, Jean, *Sensory Integration and the Child.* Los Angeles: Western Psychological Service, 2005.

Biel, Linsey, and Nancy Peske. *Raising a Sensory Smart Child.* New York: Penguin, 2005.

Bos, Bev. *Together We're Better.* Roseville, CA: Turn the Page Press, 1990.

———. *Infants and Mothers: Differences in Development.* New York: Dell, 1983.

Brazelton, Berry, and J. Sparrow. *Touchpoints 3–6.* Minneapolis, MN: Da Capo, 2002.

Brown, Stuart, and Christopher Vaughan. *Play.* Knoxville, TN: Avery, 2009.

Church, Ellen Booth. *50 Fun and Easy Brain-Based Activities for Young Learners.* New York: Scholastic Press, 2008.

Coleman, Mary, and Laura Krueger. *Play and Learn.* Roseville, MN: AbleNet, 1999.

Dennison, Paul, Ph.D. and Gail E. Dennison. *Brain Gym.* Binghamton, NY: Edu-Kinesthetics, 1992.

Fraiberg, Selma. *The Magic Years.* New York: Scribner, 1996.

Frick, Sheila, Ron Frick, Patricia Oetter, and Eileen Richter. *Out of the Mouths of Babes.* Grapevine, TX: Southpaw Enterprises, 1998.

Frith, Uta. *Autism: Explaining the Enigma.* New York: Blackwell, 1989.

Gardner, Howard. *Multiple Intelligences: The Theory in Practice.* New York: Basic Books, 1991.

Goldman, Daniel. *Emotional Intelligence.* New York: Bantam, 1995.

———. *Thinking in Pictures.* New York: Vintage, 2006.

Grandin, Temple. *The Way I See It.* Arlington, TX: Future Horizon, 2008.

Grandin, Temple, and Margaret Scariano. *Emergence: Labeled Autistic.* New York: Warner Books, 1996.

Hartmann, Thom. *Attention Deficit Disorder: A Different Perception.* Lancaster, PA: Underwood-Miller, 1993.

———. *Tool Chest.* Glendale, AZ: Henry OT Services, 2005.

Gray, Carol. *The New Social Story Book*. Arlington, TX: Future Horizons, 2000.

Greenspan, Stanley, and Nancy Thorndike Greenspan. *First Feelings*. New York: Penguin, 1989.

Greenspan, Stanley, and Nancy Lewis. *The Growth of the Mind*. Cambridge, MA: Da Capo, 1998.

———. *Building Healthy Minds*. Cambridge, MA: Da Capo, 2000.

Greenspan, Stanley, and Jacqueline Salmon. *The Challenging Child*. Cambridge, MA: Da Capo, 1998.

Greenspan, Stanley, and Robin Simons. *The Child with Special Needs*. Cambridge, MA: Da Capo, 1998.

Greenspan, Stanley, and S. Wieder. *Infancy and Early Childhood Mental Health*. New York: American Psychiatric Association, 2005.

———. *Engaging Autism*. Cambridge, MA: Da Capo Lifelong Book, 2006.

Heller, Sharon. *Too Loud, Too Bright, Too Fast*. New York: Harper, 2003.

Henry, Diana. *Tools for Tots*. Glendale, AZ: Henry OT Services, 2006.

Hickman, Lois, and Rebecca Hutchins. *Seeing Clearly*. Las Vegas, NV: Sensory Resources, 2002.

Hicks, Ester, and Jerry Hicks. *Ask and It Is Given*. Carlsbad, CA: Hay House, 1997.

Kranowitz, Carol. *The Out-Of-Sync Child Has Fun*. New York: Perigee Trade, 2003.

Kranowitz, Carol, and Lucy Miller. *The Out-of-Sync Child*. New York: Perigee Trade, 1998.

Kranowitz, Carol, and Joyce Newman. *The Out-of-Sync Child: Recognizing and Coping with Sensory Integration Dysfunction*. New York: Perigee Trade, 2009.

Levine, Mel. *A Mind at a Time*. New York: Simon & Schuster, 2002.

Miller, Lucy, and Doris Fuller. *Sensational Kids: Hope and Help for Children with Sensory Processing Disorder*. New York: Perigee, 2007.

Montagu, Ashley. *Touching: The Human Significance of the Skin*. New York: Free Press, 1993.

Montessori, Maria. *The Absorbent Mind*. Oxford, UK: Clio Press, 1994.

Piaget, Jean. *Origins of Intelligence*. New York: Norton, 1963.

Sher, Barbara. *Extraordinary Play with Ordinary Things*. Whitethorn, CA: Bright Baby Books, 1992.

———. *Self-Esteem Games*. New York: Wiley, 1997.

———. *Spirit Games*. New York: Wiley, 2002.

———. *Smart Play*. New York: Wiley, 2004.

———. *Attention Games*. New York: Wiley, 2006.

———. *Playful Moments*. Whitethorn, CA: Bright Baby Books, 2009.

———. *Homegrown Babies*. Whitethorn, CA: Bright Baby Books, 2009.

Stillman, William. *The Soul of Autism*. Franklin Lakes, NJ: New Page Books, 2008.

Taylor, Jill. *Stroke of Insight*. New York: Plume, 2009.

Trott, Maryann Colby, Marci K. Laurel, and Susan L. Windeck. *SenseAbilities: Understanding Sensory Integration*. San Antonio, TX: Therapy Skill Builders, 1993.

Williams, Donna. *Nobody, Nowhere*. New York: Avon, 1994.

———. "How Does Your Engine Run?" in *A Leader's Guide to the Alert Program for Self-Regulation*. Albuquerque, NM: Therapy Works, 1994.

Williams, Mary Sue, and Sherry Shellenberger. *Take Five! Staying Alert at Home and School*. Albuquerque, NM: Therapy Works, 2001.